LANDFALL 246

November 2023

Editor Lynley Edmeades

Reviews Editor David Eggleton
Founding Editor Charles Brasch (1909–1973)

Cover: Ann Shelton, *The loss of the oracle (cornflower, cyanus, bluebottle, bluet, bluebow, blue cap, bachelor's buttons, hurtsickle),* 2022, archival pigment print on Hahnemühle Bamboo, 840 x 1119mm.

Published with the assistance of Creative New Zealand.

OTAGO UNIVERSITY PRESS

CONTENTS

- 4 Kathleen Grattan Poetry Award 2023 Judge's Report, *Anne Kennedy*
- 5 Landfall Essay Competition 2023 Judge's Report, *Lynley Edmeades*
- 8 A Jigsaw of Broken Things, *Siobhan Harvey*
- 20 Scout's Honour, *Bronte Heron*
- 21 Root System, *Bronte Heron*
- 23 Anei anō he rā, *Robert Sullivan*
- 24 My Own Personal Marama, *Robert Sullivan*
- 25 Saturday Mornings, *Anna Scaife*
- 27 softfall, *Janet Charman*
- 28 Ten Ways to Arrive in a New Place, *Lynn Jenner*
- 30 Tōtara Trees, *Lynn Jenner*
- 31 Slightly Mourning, *Lynn Jenner*
- 32 The Sisters, *Vincent O'Sullivan*
- 39 Whose Hearts the Size of Plums?, *Rebecca Ball*
- 40 His Mouth Is His Heart, *Breton Dukes*
- 42 Ngaro Huruhuru/Native Bees, *Jenny Powell*
- 43 Hoiho, *Jenny Powell*
- 44 No Hands, *Madeleine Fenn*
- 48 Troubled Land, *Tony Beyer*
- 50 Site, *Tony Beyer*
- 51 Case Notes, *Aimee-Jane Anderson-O'Connor and Eliana Gray*
- 55 Raglan, *Brett Cross*
- 57 Veranda or Verandah, *Elizabeth Smither*
- 58 Everything Could Take, *Holly Fletcher*
- 59 Divisions, *Holly Fletcher*
- 60 Higher Lands, *Victor Billot*
- 61 Solum, *Pam Morrison*
- 62 Old West Coast Road, *Mark Edgecombe*
- 63 Not Over Dinner, *Marjory Woodfield*
- 64 ART PORTFOLIO, *Ann Shelton*
- 73 The Three Fates, *Pip Adam*
- 81 The Previous Assistant, *Pip Robertson*
- 87 Actual Forever, *Phoebe Wright*
- 89 Sons of God, *Danny Bultitude*
- 91 Mātātā | Fernbird, *Megan Kitching*
- 93 Glennie, *Kirstie McKinnon*
- 94 What the Universe Can Do for You, *Rebecca Reader*
- 100 Intersect, *Carolyn McCurdie*
- 101 The Monty Hall Problem, *Jordan Hamel*
- 103 Motherlove, *Lucinda Birch*
- 111 Secateurs, *Mary Macpherson*

112 ART PORTFOLIO, *Wayne Youle*
121 This Place Could Be Beautiful, *Frankie McMillan*
122 When I first met my grandmother, *Gail Ingram*
123 Pacific Sea Surface Temperature Anomalies, *Erik Kennedy*
124 At Puretu's Place, *Jessica Le Bas*
125 Putting the Cat Down, *Bronwyn Polaschek*
130 A Matter of Air, *Cindy Botha*
131 Shadow, *Kathryn van Beek*
139 Not Chickens, *Tessa Sinclair Scott*
140 summer, *Rachel Faleatua*
141 Lena Likes, *Petra Nyman*
145 After Reading Eleanor Catton's Birnam Wood, *David Eggleton*
146 Four Haiku for My Son, *Catherine Trundle*
147 Dawn Net, *Catherine Trundle*
148 Untitled, *Mackenzie Smith*
149 geoglyphs, *Mackenzie Smith*
150 You Knew, *Reihana Robinson*
151 The Immaculate (after Schumann), *Cadence Chung*
152 The Rose-bearer, *Cadence Chung*
153 Casanova's Shirt, *Marisa Cappetta*
154 Intruders, *Christopher Yee*
160 a (s)mothering a dunking a beating, *Sophia Wilson*
162 Fumer Tue!, *Therese Lloyd*
164 Sex and Hummus, *Jessica Arcus*
165 Spring Pudding, *Zoë Meager*
166 Anecdote of the Erotic, *Medb Charleton*
167 Caselberg Trust International Poetry Prize 2023 Judge's Report, *Rhian Gallagher*
169 Aloneness, *Tim Saunders*
170 The Tiriti Translator, *Jilly O'Brien*
172 The Time of the Wetlands, *Megan Kitching*

THE LANDFALL REVIEW
174 Landfall Review Online: Books recently reviewed / 175 EMMA GATTEY on *Te Kaihau | The Windeater* by Keri Hulme; and *Dick Seddon's Great Dive and Other Stories* by Ian Wedde / 180 WENDY PARKINS on *Laughing at the Dark* by Barbara Else / 183 HELEN WATSON WHITE on *Always Going Home – Lauris and Frances Edmond: A mother and daughter story* by Frances Edmond / 187 JOHN GERAETS on *Face to the Sky* by Michele Leggott; *Letter to 'Oumuamua* by James Norcliffe; and *A Lack of Good Sons* by Jake Arthur / 190 IAIN SHARP on *Say I Do This* by C.K. Stead; and *Respirator: A Poet Laureate Collection 2019–2022* by David Eggleton

202 CONTRIBUTORS
208 LANDFALL BACKPAGE, *Steven Junil Park*

ANNE KENNEDY

Kathleen Grattan Poetry Award 2023 Judge's Report

I'd like to congratulate all the poets who submitted their manuscripts to the Kathleen Grattan Poetry Award 2023. I found myself constantly delighted and amazed by the ideas, sounds and shapes that had gone into these collections. I could hear the poet's voice in every single one and felt huge respect for the poets and their writings—not to mention the work, passion and risk that goes into putting together a full-length collection.

It was a challenging task to choose which manuscripts reached me the most. Several of the unplaced submissions felt very promising, and I hope poets will keep drafting and inventing, and of course submitting poems to journals and other poetry platforms.

I'm very pleased to have selected as the winner 'Blue Hour' by **Jo McNeice**.

'Blue Hour' is a collection of poems that tells the journey of a woman searching among the images and events of her life for answers—sometimes finding them, sometimes not. The central theme of mental health feels strong and immediate, yet the poems dance in different ways, giving a visceral and nuanced sense of a life.

The poet searches among the means of poetry to unfold a moving story. A Gothic/fairytale edge is juxtaposed interestingly with a recognisable contemporary world. The voice here is beautiful yet unsettling, aching yet funny, lyric yet gritty. 'Blue Hour' is constructed in such a way that fragments, memories and allusions circle and surge, build and resound. It feels as if the poet is reaching across an almost impossible divide to show the reader *what it's like*.

Each time I read 'Blue Hour', I discovered more, was surprised more, yet kept coming home to the rich and challenging centre of this work.

The following submissions were shortlisted, and each impressed me for their scope, vision and originality: 'Song of the Vowels' by **Brian Flaherty**; 'A Year of Seasons' by **Saradha Koirala**; and 'Wearing Today' by **Wes Lee**.

LYNLEY EDMEADES

Landfall Essay Competition 2023 Judge's Report

It does not feel like a year since I judged my first *Landfall* essay competition, a task that simply does not get easier. Entries to this year's competition almost doubled from 2022, with a record 122 submissions. Rotating stacks of these numbered, anonymised entries were lugged from office to bedside, kitchen table to café, couch to child's sick-bed, and slowly whittled down to a long long-list, a short long-list, and an almost short-list, until I just couldn't chip away any further. The final ten essays, all place-getters in this year's competition, are the crystalline result of what must be thousands of collective hours of thinking, writing, editing and reading. It's no surprise that the best work to float to the surface were those essays that demanded reading and re-reading, a testament to the amount of time that went into them in the first place.

 Trying to find a winner in a competition like this is such a futile task. Sure, they're all essays, but the remit of the essay itself is so vast and varied that the final judgement is like posing a question as hackneyed as, is this apple better than that orange? Out of necessity, I formed categories upon which to base my judgement: a subject matter pertinent to a current national conversation (as stated by the competition's founder, Chris Price); an original and stimulating exploration of the essay form; and finally, an exposé of the writer's craft, whichever aesthetic path that took. Some essays were extraordinarily germane in their interrogation of our current cultural climate, but were less inclined to perform something original in form and craft. On the other hand, some entries were exceptionally well crafted and stretched the bounds of the essay's limits, but didn't quite have as much to 'say'.

 The winner was the essay that, after holding it up to various lights—reading it silently in bed or at the desk, or aloud while standing at the kitchen bench or pacing the room—hit all three markers with the most artistry and grace.

Siobhan Harvey's 'A Jigsaw of Broken Things' is a beautifully crafted and timely comment on prejudice against the LGBTQi+ community. While the essay doesn't pin itself to Aotearoa specifically, we don't have to go far to imagine the implications of binaristic thinking for our own queer population, especially in light of the very recent election. Harvey contemplates the current waves of discrimination against the rainbow community, wondering if we may have been so focused on progress (same-sex marriage, parenting and adoption rights, anti-discrimination laws, gender-affirming legislation, for example) that we have failed to see how 'others have been secretly working against this'. Harvey holds this contemporary issue in view while also weaving in her own story, one ultimately fraught with a failure to be accepted into her family because of the 'contamination' inherent to her 'unlovable' self. The essay picks apart the fragments of memory, experience, and pain that make up a life like this, and performs the same kind of failure that lies behind the painfully reductive attempt to *pick up the pieces*. The essay succeeds in its failure, as it were—it performs its own psychoanalytic reading of a self that has been damaged by a world obsessed with purity and appearance and, ultimately, finds solace in 'fragility and disorder'. Harvey's final comments are twofold: the writer realises, through this pain, that the hallmarks of memory—'volatility and intensity, instability and unreliability, fragility and disorder'—are also the traits that the writer uses to hone their craft. Literature as power, the proverbial middle finger to the bigotry of conservatism.

Language-as-power was also strong in the competition's runner-up, **Tīhema Baker**'s powerful 'New Zealander of the Year'. It is a kick-in-the-gut story of the author seeking fluency in te reo Māori at a full-immersion Kura Reo, where—yes, even there—the white ego continues to call the shots; a Pākehā woman, fluent in te reo, 'shamelessly flaunts a tongue steeped in the language beaten out of [his] grandfather', implicitly belittling the author for 'not being Māori enough'.

The highly-commended essays all haunted me for different reasons: **Liz Breslin**'s innovative erasure essay for what was hidden behind her feminist musings; **Hannah August**'s acerbic comment on the implications of intellectual tall-poppy syndrome (still very alive on these shores); **Pennie Hunt**'s meditation on the sad state of property ownership in New Zealand and the twisted pain of finally getting on the property ladder through the inheritance of a dead mother's assets; and **Jillian Sullivan**'s intimate rumination on dementia, where French philosophy and poetry adorn the hills of a small central Otago town.

For all its labour, judging this competition was an immense privilege and I am grateful to all the entrants for committing their thoughts and vulnerabilities to the page. The competition was stiff, and the overall quality extraordinarily high. The essay, I can decisively declare, is abound in Aotearoa.

First place
Siobhan Harvey, 'Jigsaw of Broken Things'

Second place
Tīhema Baker, 'New Zealander of the Year'

Highly commended
Liz Breslin, 'She stuck to the wheel well'
Hannah August, 'I am here to tell you that someone was'
Pennie Hunt, 'Ghost House'
Jillian Sullivan, 'Because I'm reading Cendra'

Commended
Sylvan Spring, 'Bright Mystery'
Kathryn van Beek, 'The Swiss Wolf'
Joseph Trinidad, 'Bad Language'
Anne Marie Basquin, 'Choosing Sides'

SIOBHAN HARVEY

A Jigsaw of Broken Things

Memory is set up to use the past to imagine the future—Daniel Schacter

one, part of a larger puzzle
Let me piece this together, scattered as it is across the lifespan of my memory. As if, little by little, I can make it into something complete. Even though, quite often, my memories seem like an array of singular parts. Irregular fragments belonging to a brainteaser: some with holes in them, some with loops, some one-sided, some double-edged.

    A cruel exchange between those supposedly related to one another; the random discovery of something meaningful in a difficult place; an intolerant dogma linked to a loner's fractured sense of identity; an image of broken learning; a severed relationship; a final failure to connect: this and that, replicated over and over again. Apparently disconnected. Or apparently not.

                                              &

two, irregular
I was 16 years old when my father told me no one would ever love me.

    'No one will ever love you,' he said. Offered with that deep delivery of his, as if something belonging to darkness—or something coupled to it, like a night terror—was trapped in his throat.

    Trapped in my memory also, the day I came out.

    That's all it took for the room in which we stood to narrow like his eyes.

    This, too, I recall: the day he gave oxygen to his words, a dry heat scorched the air, the room tightening so much, I felt the breath leave my body, and everything about me seemed myopic in that place I blindly thought of as home. While my mother sat in a chair nearby, watching me and my constriction with the same indifference she devoted to episodes of *Dynasty*.

    Pained, I knew my father laid bare his feelings about love and me because he passionately believed that I needed to be rescued from a future in which I'd be unloved. By others. By him.

&

three, a hole
A scatter of articles lies before me. 'Oslo shooting near gay bar investigated as terrorism, as Pride parade cancelled.'[1] 'Colorado gay club shooting suspect charged with hate crime.'[2] 'Italian government tells Milan to stop registering same-sex couples' children.'[3] 'Ugandan MPs pass bill imposing death penalty for homosexuality.'[4] 'To change your official gender in Poland you have to sue your parents.'[5] 'Spike in online hate towards trans community after Posie Parker visit.'[6]

Reading them in the lonely, tight space of my studio, I'm puzzled. I want to tell them they don't belong here; they belong elsewhere, to an unforgiving past. A past four decades or more old when, cookie-cutter-like, prejudice against LGBTQi+ people was institutionalised. A time when governments and laws openly discriminated against us. A time when police, business, health, education and housing secretly did the same. An era when the shame associated with being gay, lesbian, bi and trans turned family members against one another. An era when non-heteronormative people carrying on with their everyday lives were subjected to intentional acts of spite.

Of course, those of us who experienced such discrimination remember it clearly, which is to say, we remember it deeply, painfully. Which is also to say, perhaps naively, we thought it just that: pained recollections lost, thankfully, to a bygone age.

But these articles say otherwise. Here is proof, they remind me, that the harm of the past has resurfaced, as if an old game, believed to be gathering dust in the closet, has been rediscovered and is being replayed.

In these snippets of reportage, I also find people who've forgotten how to love—forgotten how to remember those instances of hate first encoded four decades or more ago in the minds of those who endured them. Like me.

&

four, a loop
This memory is a cul-de-sac, a dead end attached to the network of streets where I live. A busy, small town that changes when the main employer, the meatworks, closes. Suddenly, most of the working population, including my father, is made redundant.

What remains of this memory after that?

As redundancy payments dwindle, as an increasing number of shops and small businesses fail, it becomes harder for residents to keep up appearances. Yet in the emptiness of the days, weeks and months afterwards, for those once devoted to dispatching and disassembling a carcass, appearances are all that's left. A fine cut to fret over.

That's why I remember my mother cleaning her house every day, disinfecting its floors, sanitising its surfaces and buffing its windows to a blinding sheen. Whether by example, desperation or misplaced belief, she wages war against contamination, convinced it will absolve her and her household from stain. All so the neighbours can see how spotless she is. All so they can't defile her or her dwelling with their cold-shouldering shame.

Or can they?

In that world of myopia, my memory evokes how, in a time and place of redundancy, it isn't only the fear of being outcast by those we live closest to that plagues my parents. It's more encompassing and introspective than this. The creed of appearance is absolute. It creates a fear of association in all residents, placing them at risk of tainting others and, by association, being tainted themselves. All it takes is for an individual, child or adult, to exhibit behaviour neighbours deem inappropriate, and not just the miscreant but also their family face ostracism.

For my parents, this means that the fear of rejection by their neighbours is also the fear of contamination by me.

  &

five, an edge

In reviewing articles on contemporary acts of hate against queer people, I find myself wondering if my attention has been elsewhere. I've been so focused on the progress LGBTQi+ people have made in recent decades through same-sex marriage legislation, parenting and adoption rights, anti-discrimination laws, legal recognition of affirmed gender, gender-affirming healthcare and so forth, that I've overlooked how others have been working secretly against this. So, now we've reached a point in history where measures giving legislative and social equality to the rainbow community are being eroded and erased.

That's what headlines like 'Ugandan MPs pass bill imposing death penalty for homosexuality' and 'Italian government tells Milan to stop registering same-sex couples' children' seem to reveal. For in the hostility that links them and others together, I find not just a compliment to the bigotry that appears in many of my memories but also a testament to how fragile the legacy of our misfortune is, how easily it can be unremembered.

Suddenly, I realise that this isn't only a fight between political forces, the progressive versus the conservative, with gender identity as their battleground. No, it's also a conflict over memory: its evidence and erasure; how, often, it supports us and how, sometimes, it lets us down.

&

six, one-sided
A siren breaks the silence of a dull, midwinter afternoon.

From the library window, I watch students rush to escape cold, dim classrooms. Even our teachers, coated against a stiff breeze, are bowed, half-broken, as they trudge towards their cars.

Eventually, I return to the sanctuary I've created: a small desk in this otherwise unheated and empty place. I've decorated this secluded station with the pens, pencils and textbooks needed to complete my extensive homework. Even though I know I will finish that later, in my bedroom, the door closed, at the top of the house.

Appearance, that's what this is about: my stationery and workbooks, my apparent preparedness for study. For alone in this repository of ideas, I explore. Not so much an act of evasion as of discovery. I inch carefully along the shelves, searching for something, anything that might pique my interest— occasionally, slipping a book from its storage, stroking its ornate binding, parting its covers, and losing myself inside.

The Well of Loneliness bears a peculiar authorial name, Radclyffe Hall, and even more peculiarly, a heroine named Stephen. Nearby, I find *Orlando* by Virginia Woolf. So close, these separate works seem related somehow, members of the same family. Yet, in this place of appearances, these books appear untouched.

In turn, I hold them open as I surrender to their sentences. Soon, each begins to unravel me so that in their similar and different ways, they make me feel like I've been stolen by something strange but familiar, bonded to it by word and being, yet not quite understanding this affiliation, this kindred alliance. As if, secretly stored inside, something about me is hauled by these novels into the light.

Eventually, I secrete both books into my schoolbag and carry them home.

Later, my homework complete, I traverse these books as if their chapters are stepping stones laid across some undisclosed space. The more I read, the more I feel I'm making progress.

Not an epic, swashbuckling narrative disclosed across continents and decades, but something personal, psychological and emotional. Something also about being trapped: this, *The Well of Loneliness* also imparts, is what drama can be. While *Orlando* enables me to realise that against a sweeping, historical backdrop, it's the individual—their life, mind, heart, motivations and memories—that matters most, outlasting all changes, be they temporal, cerebral or physical. In both, I perceive that someone marginalised by society can lead a life important enough to devote to the page.

&

seven, interlocking
There's a connection here. These separate things, these things fractured by time, the articles and my memories share a common bond. Be it historical or contemporary, public or private, they are linked by prejudice, yes, but also by fragility and survival.

The news stories penned by journalists around the world speak to the frailty of any advancement queer people have made in recent times, of how in some countries acts might have been introduced to legitimise and protect diverse existences, but that everywhere LGBTQi+ people continue to encounter senseless laws and senseless discrimination, hate laws and hate speech; and how, even in the face of all that, we endure.

The memories I'm summoning up are also meditations upon fault and continuity: a parent who finds stigma in six loveless words; a nobody like me who turns to the words on a page to realise themselves.

For a moment, I imagine there's a conversation here, the articles and my memories in communion about the things they share. Personified, each element unites in robust exchange, a picture of eloquent work, to which I, as a writer, am the host.

Yet something continues to trouble me, something connected still to memory, its assistance and deficit.

                                                        &

eight, double-edged
Black and white, a simple affair, my Sony ICF-38 portable radio transmits the news. This airs while I'm re-reading *The Well of Loneliness*, closing in on the provocation of its last line, 'Give us also the right to our existence.'[7]

A dramatic soundbite yields to a keynote address, something as soft and stirring as a dog whistle as an orator conjures up the innocent and the collective. Our children, that is. Then the disembodied voice speaks of its concern.

A pause.

Suddenly, bitter and broad, the voice rises, filling the space with its alarm. Concern because, the speaker explains, our vulnerable young people are at risk; so, too, are our traditional morals. The source of the menace isn't a war or a plague (not of the conventional kind, anyway) but the threat presented by those who are gay.

As I set *The Well of Loneliness* face down, as if to hide it from shame, I feel myself detained by this hard-toned assailant and their intolerant persuasion, the kind able to reach deep inside me, tear open my vitals and find fault.

Deception and contamination: these are the words the orator uses next. Along the way, they raise visions of torment as varying as the gutter, mythical purgatories like Hades, and that misunderstood thing called AIDS.

This is wrong, I tell myself: the viscera I am, the heart I own, the mind and being. Wrong, all wrong. This speech also seems to me, in my fraught teenage state, to be associated with some pervasive, mature decree. One I'm too young to deny, too powerless to expel. Transmitted as it is by a state broadcaster, I also see in it the authority that such status commands. The status, for instance, of the parent over the child.

Control, the orator concludes, relies upon the audience realising there's a deception at play. Because otherwise, the innocents are being hoodwinked out of leading a normal life by believing it's fine to be gay.

Rapturous applause follows. It bursts from my transistor and occupies my room like thunder. My young mind trembles with thoughts of injustice, for in a moment, I've been stained by someone's perception of me, and then, an atrocity, a future has been stirred up in which I'm forever outcast.

I silence the broadcast.

Below me, the house continues to reverberate with that speech played loud on the radio in the living room. Soon, I'm privy to the sound of my father's assent.

'Too bloody right, those fuckin' perverts!' Offered in that deep delivery of his, its base notes rising towards me from below. As if the house is secretly under attack. A pest, perhaps, gnawing away at the shell of our lives.

Afterwards, the impression formed from the orator's most compelling words plays on repeat in my young mind, 'Contaminated … cheated … contaminated … cheated …'

By then, darkness is at my window. I turn to face it, find the sky empty but for a silhouette of stars. Tears blur my vision. What's before me seems smeared into a half-finished photograph, a negative raw in its exposure.

                                                              &

nine, opposing

As my memories link and replicate the substance of the articles before me, I see that there's also a contrary sense of detachment about them. Simultaneous sequencing and dislocation. It's there, for instance, in the way the arrangement of my recollections displaces time. For the events of my first remembrance occurred when I was 16 years old, while those of the second and third memories took place when I was 15. This means that not only are my memories failing to line up chronologically, but in breaching time, they're also rearranging it. So that, out of sync with the principles of general relativity, my memories make possible backward time travel as if they're akin to a rotating black hole.

Here's another memorial anomaly. Why, in its nonchronological ordering, does my mind choose my father's six loveless words as a point of origin? Which is to ask, by association, why doesn't it begin elsewhere?

With me hurriedly packing my suitcase, for instance.

Or with my father silently closing the door on me.

Or the cold night I trudged unwittingly through when, alone, I looked up at a night sky empty but for a single, dead star.

Or my being swallowed by an empty bus and transported out of that redundant town.

If there's no logic to the selection of the first part of my memory puzzle, then is there any logic to my entire recall?

There's rationale, this much I know. As I reflect upon my troubles over memory, I realise they are based on undeniable fact. It's true, for example, that in the 1980s of my youth, a prominent politician gave a speech in which they attacked the right of people to be queer.

Even so, further irregularities with my memory process abound. Like its inclusion of supposition, such as, 'In this place of appearance, these books appear untouched.' Not to mention subjectivity, like, 'What's before me seems smeared into a half-finished photograph, a negative raw in its exposure.'

It's as if, in its working embracement of competing constructs of time, truth, subjectiveness and character portrayal, my memory forms a conundrum of alternate realities, a jigsaw of broken things.

                                                                             &

ten, a hole, a loop
Soon, *The Well of Loneliness* and *Orlando* disappear from the library in my faith-based school. Gone also are Alice Walker's *The Color Purple*, which was part of last year's literature curriculum, and works by Gertrude Stein, E.M. Forster, Christopher Isherwood, James Baldwin and any author whose ideas might contaminate students.

In their place, we're instructed to read William Faulkner's *As I Lay Dying* and Arthur Miller's *A View from the Bridge*.

I empathise with Miller's raw portrayal of family life, its tensions and brutalities. But quickly, I come to realise that its inclusion in my education belies a darker subtext. Our teacher directs us to analyse Eddie's obsession with Catherine, his wife's orphaned niece, as something that is wrong because it's extramarital, not because it's sexually taboo. Rodolfo's kiss with Eddie, we're told, is shameful. Eddie's twisted suspicion that Rodolfo is gay turns our teacher into a fool as he performs for us, his captive audience, this character's dialogue with limp-wristed, high-voiced affectation.

As this charade continues, I stare at the bound text before me, its words blurring into a dark cavity as I imagine what's missing. *Orlando*, for instance, and how, in its absence, I long for its return. If only to be able to find myself in its pages, and elsewhere.

  &

eleven, double loops
All this unsettlement and uncertainty found in the memories I've retrieved. All this disturbance and vulnerability found in the articles I've read.

    I see the connection. But I also see the inherent failing.

    The articles report facts. They offer no solutions and don't remind readers that their depictions of the discrimination and violence faced by queer people are nothing new. We've been here before, and we haven't learned from the past, the better to heal and not repeat it: this is what the articles erase.

    As a pattern, this is what my memories make visible. But they're limited, my internal truth. Moreover, they're made of things almost invisible and permanently short-lived. A speck of serotonin, an electrical charge so brief it can't be seen. A consequent micro-explosion that fuses across the infinitesimal space of a synapse (the junction between two neurons or nerve cells in the brain).

    So insubstantial and ephemeral are memories, it's no surprise that, like the parts of an old machine, they're liable to break down. Indeed, the many ways in which they can fail us, in which we can fail them, include absent-mindedness, apparent insignificance, repression (through disassociation), conscious suppression, senility, dementia, physical illness, psychological distress, false memory and confabulation (invention of a memory to replace an absence of recall). So, the wonder of memory isn't its existence but its survival in the face of a multitude of ways to eradicate it.

&

twelve, a hole, a loop
This is a memory I've tried to forget. A memory that turns in on itself, spinning everything about me, about the people who raise me, into an emptiness so vast it engulfs all the axioms and lies about family I once thought were true. Like, family is everything. Like, family always loves you, no matter what. Yes, all the truisms related to relatives we construct our lives and society upon, swallowed, and therein, in this memory, I'm swallowed too.

    For after my parents estrange me, I still believe it's my fault. Family are always there to support and love one another; mine just need a little time to get used to my coming out. So, in this memory, emboldened by the lie of the season, a time of professed goodwill to all, I retrace my steps back to my parents' home one December evening a decade or so after that politician's speech about being deceived.

Although I find the cul-de-sac warm and veiled in humidity, in that place where appearances matter, it appears as if nothing has changed. A blind alley, each dwelling staring back at the other, keeping its inhabitants in check.

Soon enough, darkness creeps in. Around me, net curtains twitch with a stealth worthy of someone releasing the safety mechanism on a gun. I feel the intuitive warning signals, the vulnerable experience when they sense disquiet: my ears burn; my spine tingles.

For a second, I'm conflicted by my closeness to the people who raised me, rejected me. Self; and ghosted other. Returned to where I came from; and free of this.

To keep myself occupied, I imagine something else: inside the edifice of the house where I grew up, strangers rise early; there's a gathering in the name of family; there are offerings of benevolence and gifts wrapped with messages of love; finally, a prayer, 'For what we are about to receive, may the Lord make us truthful thankful …' blesses a special meal.

When I knock at the door, I see a figure rise behind frosted glass.

I call out a greeting.

Breaking their advance, the figure halts, turns its back, then disappears.

I wait in case there has been an error. Perhaps my knocking has gone unheard. Perhaps my presence has gone unnoticed.

Further minutes of disregard elapse in that oppressive heat, where the humidity is so stifling it makes movement difficult. Throughout, I sense the neighbours and their net twitching at my back, the creed of appearance still absolute in their dead end.

Finally, I withdraw, and never return.

&

thirteen, double-edged again
A jigsaw of broken things: memories; people; time. A family broken, in memory and time, by puzzlement over identity. The conundrums that continued after the utterance of six loveless words, to encode my existence.

There in my subsequent homelessness and poverty. There in my ongoing nightmares. There in a series of failed relationships, a string of failed jobs. All of that, all of this, there inside me, an unstoppable engine driven by guilt. Guilt I couldn't be a better child, the kind the people who raised me would never reject.

Guilt and recollection: the spark of one igniting the other in me. Like two nerve cells forging an explosive link.

&

fourteen, all loops
Volatile and intense; unstable and unreliable; nonlinear and subjective; random and selective: this, I've come to understand, is the nature of memory.

What, then, of my attempt to figure out how, piece by piece, recollections of intimate discrimination and estrangement might correlate to the prejudice found in the recent articles I've amassed?

The fragility and disorder: on the surface, my memories appear to create more problems than answers. I should feel let down by them. A parent disappointed by their offspring.

But I don't.

Volatile and intense; unstable and unreliable; nonlinear and subjective; random and selective; fragile and disordered: if these are the hallmarks of memory and its inner workings, the writer in me also sees they are the hallmarks of creativity and its inner workings. In all forms, artistry is about being inspired by, employing and refining the volatility and intensity, instability and unreliability, randomness and selectiveness, fragility and disorder inherent in the drive towards the completion of new work. These components aren't hindrances standing in the way of my writing about them. No, they're part of a process that, little by little, concludes a creative work.

&

end piece
My dilemma is resolved. Memories, articles and my associated thinking: these, I know now, I can sequence as a creative thing that, as a whole, might build a picture of something resonant to the present. In doing so, in their own small way, my memories might offer testimony, one of the many needed to enable us as a society to remember that our differences over identity are

longstanding, divisive and, therein, still need to be resolved.

Addressing an empty page, my pen begins its task,

one, part of a larger puzzle

Let me piece this together, scattered as it is across the lifespan of my memory. As if little by little, I can make it into something complete …

---

1   Jessie Yeung, Mayumi Maruyama, James Frater, Niamh Kennedy, Sarah Diab and Li-Lian Ahlskog Hou, 'Oslo shooting near gay bar investigated as terrorism, as Pride parade cancelled'. CNN, 24 June 2022. https://edition.cnn.com/2022/06/24/europe/norway-oslo-gay-bar-shooting-intl-hnk/index.html
2   Colleen Slevin, 'Colorado gay club shooting suspect charged with hate crime'. Stuff, 7 December 2022.https://www.stuff.co.nz/world/us-canada/300758659/colorado-gay-club-shooting-suspect-charged-with-hate-crimes
3   Federico Maccioni, 'Italian government tells Milan to stop registering same-sex couples' children'. Reuters, 15 March 2023. https://www.reuters.com/world/europe/italian-government-tells-milan-stop-registering-same-sex-couples-children-2023-03-14/
4   Samuel Okiror, 'Ugandan MPs pass bill imposing death penalty for homosexuality'. The Guardian, 21 March 2023). https://www.theguardian.com/world/2023/mar/21/ugandan-mps-pass-bill-imposing-death-penalty-homosexuality
5   Anna Gmiterek-Zablocka, 'To change your official gender in Poland you have to sue your parents'. Notes from Poland, 31 March 23. https://notesfrompoland.com/2023/03/31/to-change-your-official-gender-in-poland-you-have-to-sue-your-parents-causing-trauma-for-trans-people/
6   Hamish Cardwell, 'Spike in online hate towards trans community after Posie Parker visit'. RNZ, 4 April 2023. https://www.rnz.co.nz/news/national/487306/spike-in-online-hate-toward-trans-community-after-posie-parker-visit-researchers
7   Radclyffe Hall, The Well of Loneliness (Virago, 1996), p. 447.

BRONTE HERON

Scout's Honour

Probably rabid J. thinks We have to figure out how to deal with it
and by deal I mean One of those tasks like trapping mice
or buying a fridge In Prospect Park I saw a mockingbird perched
on one of the nearby branches I could tell by his long tail and his light
grey body He kept escaping from the view of the binoculars No
the correct word is flit To flit is the nature of the bird and by seeking
it I conform to his nature My neck twitching left and right in poor
mimicry The raccoon balances along the top of the fence
seemingly unworried then onto the roof Consider the dog
how she trains her gaze on the birds her muscles taut Her instinct
is predatory When Atticus Finch stood in the street with his gun
pointed at that rabid mutt he held his arm out straight

Root System

A word is about to burst forth
It presses against its thin chrysalis The tongue pulls
back into the throat to make room for the blossoming that will soon take
place Muted purple deepening inside the gummy pink chamber of the mouth
and then the breaking open
                                              orchid
Pushing up from the hard ground The circular passage of the mouth
as a breath travels from the base of the chest through the wind-
pipe The low pitch of it leaving
the body The mind is aware
of the flower's form I can see the long stem curving to hold
the heart-shaped petals the complex opening of its centre When I say it again
the noun breaks in two
cut down the middle by its arrangement of consonants I repeat
myself The bifurcation of thalli and axial organs
creating new varieties The plant breathes
with my lungs as I cast its seeds out into the world They scatter
as meaning does when a word is said over and over
I turn the word over
unearthing my first pronunciations Myself as a nine-year-old
learning to read my small body bent over a series of marks
as they appear on the page They signify a flower made of invisible material
that when brought to the front of the mouth feels like
                                          orchard as the tongue
hits the back of the teeth then curls
up towards the soft palate When I say orchard I conjure a field of purple
blanketed by a glottal frost Literacy as a series of layers that cover
verbal instinct Those first sounds composted under the succeeding ones
to allow for the redistribution of letters

word-molecules that float
like noise as they re-order themselves I say
                              awkward to feel them
collide grimacing in anticipation The word is not cut cleanly
in half but rather broken up into uneven chunks clusters of the incorrect
drifting farther away from their origin Spore-like
thick-walled and insistent
as they land inside the freshly opened bulbs They stick to the stigmatic
surface of the orchid held out to taste
Time passes as a series of bitter images The orchid grows awkwardly
through light as it changes lifting its head to the sun
and bowing into the night This movement a form of breath
a synthesis of process I stand in the field as it thaws
inhaling the purple air   orchid
of multiple   orchis
plant bodies   orkhis Queerness
of the plant-body as it grows someplace other than sex It desires
only the most basic requirements for living I kneel to breathe in the scent
sweet rot of matter green
waste feeding the new The flower eats through the organ of its skin Its pores
open to receive nutrients I pause inside this image Peeling back a layer
of the real I dig my hands into
the hush of dirt to touch the pre-verbal The temperature is cooler
here It calms the anxiety of speech the fear of falling
inside a sentence Language arranges itself
inside of me reorienting to this silence Words lose their descriptive use
serving only as sound Letters fragment and move
freely their edges coming up against each other every now and then
they make a muffled clicking when they meet I push further into the dirt
and thought recedes The body continues
to grow from the place the hands are planted

ROBERT SULLIVAN

Anei anō he rā

I've folded Uenuku up into my pāua shell studded
writing book and started whistling the Kermit the frog song
again, 'Why are there so many songs about rainbows?'
Sometimes I use my uncarved koauau
which sounds just like my whistling
but I'm sure I'm blowing and not puckering.
It was a jazz waiata when I first brought out
my un-koauau, and reached out for hugs
made of Miles Davis brass. Now I know that to believe
in aroha, or love, is honourable and plain,
no similes for it except to say that love
has a purpose. Sure, I see things that remind me
of love, such as the gold over snow-capped mountains,
and the gold in fields of spring, and the gold
in dripping kōwhai blossoms that look sweet.
But they don't measure up really.
They're compensation. Those images are ideas
and lack the bite, kaha te katakata kicks and lick of life.

My Own Personal Marama

'Marama. Ko Marama tērā,'
I'd say and point up there. I told him

about Rona and the tī kōuka too.
Then I'd go and sit on the moon,

lifted by moths to sing from my
cabbage tree not unlike a little prince,

or David Bowie. I go up there and waiata
like it's 1999, cloaked in shuffling wings,

watching Papatūānuku from the sky—
change into a glittering pāua in space

to marvel at the sea, my whānau,
and being a piri pāua, at my home.

ANNA SCAIFE

Saturday Mornings

Merrin couldn't find the manila folder that contained my notes. She searched through the piles on her desk, and I hovered on the edge of the office couch and waited. A week before, at our first appointment, she'd asked about my childhood home. I paused, pinching my lip between my thumb and forefinger, so she could see I was thinking about her question.

'There was me, my older brother, and my parents. I think our family was ordinary, except for not being allowed to watch TV,' I said.

She raised both eyebrows, poised her ballpoint over the notepad. I thought that meant I should keep talking. I hoped so—I didn't want her to think I was one of those women who go on.

I told her, 'Dad was worried my brother and I would become addicts. We had a television—a black and white set with legs. They kept it in the lounge, but she turned it around to face the wall.'

'She?'

'My mother.'

'Why do you think she did that?'

'I don't know, Feng Shui maybe,' I said.

'I see,' she said, but I don't think she wrote it down.

Merrin found the folder with my notes near the bottom of the pile. She should have a better system, I thought. If it was me, I would pull out the files and stack them in order of the appointments.

'Sorry about that, I'm a bit disorganised today,' she said, settling into her chair.

'Don't tell me,' I said, 'I'm exactly the same.'

She looked down at her notebook. 'Last week we talked about your family home. Today I'd like you to try and describe how it was for you living there.'

My father's chickens stopped laying. Dad gave those hens time to redeem themselves. He gave them more chances than most people would. There were two with brown and black feathers, two white with blood-red combs and this little speckled bantam named Shoo. When you cracked Shoo's eggs into the frying pan, the bright yolks were the size of ten cent pieces.

'Get in there early to collect the eggs,' Dad said. 'Those chooks will all go broody otherwise.' They never did, but later they stopped laying altogether. Dad couldn't work it out. I saw him reading his book, *Keeping Backyard Chickens*. Bent over, smoothing his fine hair across the top of his head and muttering, 'I'm doing that. It's not that.'

He wrung their necks on a Saturday morning. My mother called us to come inside and stand facing the wall with our backs to the kitchen window. The washing machine chugged and lurched in the corner. I picked at the cracks in the paint, made stripes with my toe in a pile of spilled flour on the linoleum. Then my mother said, 'Right, that's done. You can go now.' My father let himself in the back door, his shirt sleeves rolled up and his forehead creased. My mother turned to the bench and sank her hands into the dishwater.

Living there was like standing with the tip of my nose against the green paint on our kitchen wall.

That was not the story I told Merrin. I told her about holidays, our family dog, the time my brother towed me behind his bike on my roller skates and I grazed the skin off my leg from hip to ankle.

I didn't tell her that for weeks after the chickens died my father took his dinner and a folding chair out to the garden and ate there alone, or that my mother packed an overnight bag and stayed away for two months.

After that she covered the television with a tablecloth and placed a lamp on top. My brother and I sneaked under its white linen skirt and pressed the unresponsive buttons.

A woman from her gardening club remarked, 'What a good idea, covering up the goggle box. You should see my boys on a Saturday morning. They're glued to it.'

My mother said, 'Don't tell me. My two are exactly the same.'

JANET CHARMAN

softfall

we walked in Kabul
along that sunny boulevard
below the prison mountain
me tied in my lava lava—skinny as
dusty hair scarfed
and only a step ahead of you in your
rainbow-stripe sun-frock

so i didn't see it
when in passing us
a local male grabbed you by the genitals

any man anywhere might do that
—he doesn't have to be the president

your shock i felt
and your disgust mixed with relief
that from a stranger male
you'd
been dealt the imprimatur of the authentic feminine
—abjection

you who'd never menstruated
or had breasts
my becoming stranger friend
growing daily less and less dismayed to cherish
what you called your Adonis physique
and with whom jointly i re-lived your late
pre-birth
in those three months we camped across the earth

LYNN JENNER

Ten Ways to Arrive in a New Place

I
The rules say that we should take into account as many independent judgements as we can muster. And that we should acquaint ourselves with the statistical probability of various outcomes. And furthermore, that we should make our decision in surroundings where we feel comfortable and safe.

II
All of this suggests that we should make our decision in our own home, surrounded by piles of books and empty coffee cups. We should both have our devices open: his showing a spreadsheet of our household budget and mine a set of graphs showing the likelihood of a global recession, the probable result of the next election and house values in six territorial areas.

III
The risk is that if a decision is made while you are out of your regular environment and your company is anything but independent in its outlook you are almost certain to leap toward vivid possibilities. We were in a friend's kitchen when it happened. Someone put forward a novel suggestion. Oh yes, we said. That makes sense. The result will be rare and wonderful. Then we forgot about the spreadsheet and put our money down.

IV
I am surprised and angry to find that in the new place certain conversations are only for men. I have far too many woollen coats but no gumboots and no work boots. I don't know whether to treat four wet days in a row like a little holiday or try to be productive in some indoor way.

V
All the vegetables taste sweeter than they used to. The fish we eat has been caught the day before and our neighbours give us bowls of pale blue eggs.

VI
One day someone asks me what all my books are for. Another day someone asks me if I make much money from my writing. I look at my phone a lot. I read the entire works of Georgette Heyer. Some books more than once. It becomes more and more difficult to sustain the pretence of joy or even normalcy.

VII
Some part of me keeps slipping away to a stucco house of the softest desert pink that hovers upside down, on the horizon.

VIII
After a year it comes to me that Georgette Heyer might not be helping. I swear off Regency romances. I meet regularly with other writers. They all create poems and stories but I have nothing to say.

IX
I make a blanket for my bed. All I have to do is make the same stitch a thousand times. Then comes zucchini pickle because pickle goes with everything. Then marmalade, made from fruit given to me in a carpark by a woman I had never met before. This act of kindness seems to be of this place.

X
Then comes strawberry jam because my mother said you must grab the moment. After the strawberry jam come two apple cakes. After the apple cakes, I read the new collection from Louise Glück which has been on my table for half a year. After that, I find I have something to say about tōtara trees.

Tōtara Trees

A man called Leo makes white porcelain no thicker than an eggshell. You find yourself lifting a cup and when you hold it up to the light, you see your own hand. One day he says he thinks the things a man can make are more beautiful than nature, and I say no, that cannot be. Then Leo says books are more profound than nature. I am shocked. Of course. But now this crazy comparison is in my mind. On the one hand, a single book. On the other, a stand of tōtara trees, each as tall as a church. In the end, every book tells you that life is made up of pain and uncertainty and relentless work, Leo says. Trees only tell you that light can be green, and that a hundred years is both a short and a long time. I tell Leo that trees tell me to breathe more deeply. Yes, he says. You should read more Russians.

Slightly Mourning

Today, in the pages of Speak Memory I found a note I had left myself some years ago. Mauve, it said, was Vladimir Nabokov's favourite colour.

And I thought about a mauve dress I once bought from a second-hand shop. I wore that dress to the funeral of my husband's grandmother—a woman I never met, but a good Catholic woman, the priest said.

And my husband sat there angry, his arms all stiff and pointy because his grandmother was more than a dutiful woman who attended Mass every Sunday and helped with the flowers.

And she'd had a hard life, my husband said, married for fifty years to a bad-tempered man and never any money. She sent us a pair of cheap orange and yellow floral sheets for our wedding—they were already out of fashion and I never put them on the bed. And now that family violence is not okay, I wonder if her bad-tempered husband knocked her around.

And after the Mass we stood in the icy rain while they put her back into the ground—earth to earth, person to muddy hole.

And now that I'm as old as she was when she bought the sheets, I know that mauve is the colour of half mourning—that first you wear black, then grey, then mauve, and finally white, that lightening to show that life has thrown a knife down on a person below but everyone has to continue walking, not knowing when the next knife will fall.

And Vladimir Nabokov—upon whom knives and blocks of steel and statues of prancing horses and grand pianos had fallen—had also to continue walking.

VINCENT O'SULLIVAN

The Sisters

She is dead, and I am distraught. There is nothing else I want to write back to the letters that still arrive, even weeks after I think this must, surely, be the last of them. Yet should I write that, however true it might be, it would seem almost brutally curt, or melodramatic, like saying there is nothing to touch my grief. I answer the kind condolences with one cliché after another—how I am far from being the only one who misses her, or how our seeing so little of each other as adults did not diminish our closeness. All this is true, yet inadequate enough to not seem like truth at all. I am saying what is expected of me. I am not saying, and not yet even to myself, *for the first time in my life I am free.*

Well before we were adults, and whatever else might be weighed up one way or another in comparing me with Claudine, I was the one who got things right. I looked at us both, as I looked at most things, with a clearer eye. If there was one of those disturbances that exist in any family, a crisis which was minor enough but at the time seemed the world's problem, our mother would hear Claudine out, and then ask, 'And what would you say, Audrey?' She knew the facts would be put more logically, with less emotion slopping their edges.

I'll give you an instance. When a budgie we were meant to share as a joint gift—that's trouble in the making, to begin with—died, my sister sobbed and her breath caught and she said it was an accident when we were lifting it from its cage. I knew the benefits of being brave about things. I said, 'I think its head twisted the way Claudine held it when the door was shut too early. It was no one's fault.'

'Then you should have said so, shouldn't you?' our father said when he came in from work. Claudine was the one who said sorry when we wrapped it in a piece of old teatowel and buried it with its eyes still glinty between nearly closed lids, and its claws out stiff, like it wanted to hang on.

We liked it when Dad came in from work early in the morning, rather than in the afternoon as most fathers did. He stood in his singlet at the sink in the wash-house, his shirt thrown across the washing machine, and the suds went right up his arms, washing away the white dust from the bakery. Then he would come inside and give each of us a brown paper bag with something nice he had brought us.

Claudine and I laughed about that when we met as grown-ups. Neither of us, so long after he was dead, was able to think of him apart from the smell of the soap he used, that when it was worn down from the fat slab it began as, you could see through its thin-as-thin amber clearness if you held it up. He would sit in the kitchen and one of us would ask could we make you a cup of tea, Daddy, and he would tell us, 'I'd kill for one,' which seemed a strange thing to say, even if he laughed as he said it. We loved the things he would say at times that drove our mother to slap his arm. 'Honestly, Ron, how can you expect the girls to grow up ladies if you talk like that?' Sometimes he might even lift the lid from something cooking on the stove and lick his lips at us and turn to Mum and tell her, Hungry? He could eat a nun's arse through a convent gate.

We got on well enough, Claudine and I. Once I tried to tell her, making light of it, yet never being more serious, 'It all goes back to our names, you know, Claudine. Yours was the name a fairy godmother hands out. Then *Audrey*. You hear Audrey and you think of country wenches in old books. Housewives in slippers and uncombed hair. Might as well throw in freckles, if you have me in mind.'

My sister, younger by eighteen months, laughed when we talked like this, seemingly getting on like happy sisters. But she saw through me with her almost violet eyes, their sloping slightly the way some men think irresistible. I didn't put it so directly to her, but I did in a notebook I kept at one stage much later, when I was told it could be more beneficial than you might ever think, to jot down odd things that popped into your mind. So I wrote, 'One sister like the doll off a Christmas tree, the other like a peg with a hanky tied around it, her one shot at having something of her own.' Either way, as it later became clear to me, it was really what both of us wanted—my feeling hard done by, Claudine believing it was her fault. No question that we loved each other. But love never meant other things could not shade it, where a lot more than love might put down roots.

Dad died when we were in our teens. The awful gap, for both of us, once the smell of the bakery left us, the welcome-home lathering of soap. I've mentioned the fairy godmother. When I was at university and fell for the whole business of myth, I revised that into the Fates. Spinning away, implacable. Claudine their favoured one—how could she not be? Gold hair that fell in one splendid wave, her kindness so genuine it might so easily be taken as false. The closest she came to reprimanding me was once saying, 'Trust people more, Audrey. They *want* to like you.'

I flashed through university, as my mother liked to tell people. Then, not to do her other daughter down, she would say how she was the more placid one, happy in her work with a charity organisation, flying off to the islands at different times, working for—you might have heard of him—Fred Hollows?

Much later, when our mother became ill, Claudine nursed her at home. On Sunday evenings she emailed what read more like old-fashioned letters than the quick summaries of a busy life my own emails tended to be. She felt it was the least she might do, passing on details about our mother, how she seemed, so quickly, to be drawing into herself, talking about Dad as if he'd stroll in any minute, becoming quite agitated about small things.

Claudine did her best to conceal how trying in fact it must have been for her. I know she had it fixed in her mind that my first year in a permanent position at UCL must have been a difficult time for me—'all work and no play', as she said. She also imagined that the weather 'over there' was a constant battle to keep warm, to avoid flu or worse, what you picked up in the Tube. All the problems she saw on TV.

I could have told her I was revelling in a kind of life I could not have dreamed of. I was popular with students, my book couldn't be more than a year away, there was a man who was crazy about me and another who was drop-dead gorgeous, in that dreadful phrase, who taught me to drink, and to make the most of what I had, but who went rock climbing in Wales and now was in a wheelchair at his parents' home half a day's drive from London.

Talk about the Fates. Which as any adult knows is a way of saying, well, not my fault, was it? Soon after I got to the UK I must have been looking morose when I got talking casually with an acquaintance at the local indoor pool. She asked me was I having an exciting time socially, and I said, looking wry, I hoped, 'An exciting time, what's that?' And this acquaintance said, as if doing her best for me, 'But it isn't hard to get a boyfriend early in the term, is it? They're grateful for anything—have you noticed?'

At times there's nothing to fall back on it seems but clichés. 'Time flies,' I found myself writing towards the end of each term, and now it was more than two years since I'd been back home. Our Sunday night emails, once our mother had died, slipped to one a fortnight, then to one in three weeks. I would of course have flown back for the funeral but it was summer and I had just returned from a break in Turkey and taken ill—meningitis was floated as likely. Weeks of tests and the rest of it before what was really a minor infection cleared up and by then we were into my first new teaching course since promotion. You don't realise how cut-throat academe can be.

Claudine was understanding, as she always was. I gathered there was a man she was interested in, and then another, but mostly she wrote in her matter-of-fact way of what, frankly, sounded hum-drum enough. I worried for a time when she said she had been put in charge of rostering shifts for volunteers at a kind of relief centre. Something admirable. I'm not in the least sceptical about such things, I just know I couldn't do something as worthy as that myself, and I hoped her life wasn't narrowing too much with her political views. Most of which we shared in any case. 'Claudine's the one with *principles*,' I found myself saying, if people asked me, is she anything like you? It was a smiley way of avoiding having to think of a real answer.

I could have said, but there is never any reason to answer such queries accurately, that the difference between us was that Claudine *accepted*, which is something I'd never say about myself. She accepted my excuses for not coming back for a visit, my not suggesting she come over and live with me for a while, any good news about work or travel or grants that I might send her, and mean it *absolutely*, how pleased she was for my sake.

Without intending it for a minute, she made me uneasy with myself. Not permanently, of course, but enough. Enough to rattle me a little in a curious way. One evening Claudine and I had chatted on for half an hour, her excitement genuine and mine too, after I had said this summer—*her* summer—would it be all right if we came back for a month? We hadn't actually *spoken* for ages. It was marvellous just talking together. A fortnight with her, say, in the house we had grown up in and where she still lived. And if she felt she would like to, she could join us as we travelled around the country. Jean-Paul was dead keen to see as much of it as he could.

I had scarcely put down the phone when nostalgia of a kind I seldom felt so much as a smidgin racked me. Now there's a word I'd never have thought I'd use about myself! Almost a physical hurt, the suddenness of it. I was crying when I went back to the kitchen from the study where I had been speaking with Claudine. Jean-Paul looked up, said nothing, and refilled our glasses. There was a silence as I sat next to him and leaned into his shoulder. I waited for him to touch my hair and brush his cheek against mine. I'm seldom sentimental about love but that night I was. I wanted his hands on me. I wanted to hear him lose his breath.

How often it's been said, by someone like myself, away for so long, that the shock of going back is not how things have changed, but how they have stayed the same. The two tubs of fuchsias near the front door that our mother first planted when we were at school. Can fuchsias last like that? Or were these different plants altogether? I have no idea about that kind of thing. To see the same wallpaper, the same pictures on the walls. A broad deck had been added to the back of the house, and the kitchen refashioned. There was some new furniture, but not a lot. A large-screen television. But the bedrooms were the same. The bathroom. This was merely the old touched up, rather than something fresh, which for some reason I had expected.

Of course I had made the mistake of thinking that my sister's life had somehow been on hold in my absence, which was totally wrong. She had been living, as had I in my different way, in the ordinary every day, which so quickly becomes the ordinary every year. It's a mistake we so often make thinking of those who are absent from us. We imagine them holding still, like dolls on a wardrobe shelf, until we return and open the door. How dare they seem changed from when we last closed it!

Yet for all that, as I woke in the morning and went to the bathroom with its familiar tiles, or swung back the picket gate onto the slope leading up to Ponsonby Road, there was that pressure, for a while at least, of the past that so dovetailed into this. Those moments as if I had never left. This happened especially when I opened the door of the pantry, which was left untouched when Claudine had done up the kitchen. Perhaps she was held by its nostalgia too. That smell which had never changed, its confusion of dried herbs and lavender in a vase on the high shelf, ginger and God knows what else. Even what looked like the same glass jars of preserved fruit our mother had made. Claudine said she kept that up, year by year. Nothing to do with sentimentality, just that she had never come across a better recipe than Mum's.

What got me most, now that I'm on to my 'spots of time', which I always find students so like the notion of, was the 'archway', which was what we called the rough frame Dad erected from bent tubular steel and chicken wire before I started school, the same passionfruit vine thick and gnarly across it. I liked picking the fruit when it was pale purple and fat and putting the firm globes in a dish, fascinated by how if you left them over the weeks they became wrinkled 'old people passionfruit'.

I wandered down to the little shed at the end of the back yard, flush against the neighbour's fence, and which contained nothing but a few suitcases and folded sacking, and a few tools still hanging where they were meant to be in the pencilled lines drawn around them. On the ledge inside the small window with its rusty metal clasp sat a saucer that must have been there since Dad's time, its shrivelled stain perhaps from something he had intended to grow. I found I was suddenly crying, and was terrified Claudine or Jean-Paul might see me. There was nothing I might have said that would make sense of it.

Jean-Paul was delighted to see me so contented, watching the way Claudine and I got on. He was an only child and I could tell how, in the nicest way, he envied us. He liked being with the two of us, but knew how precious this time was and was marvellously considerate. He threw himself into the city and must have walked miles every day, surprised, I think, that the country was not as rough-grained as he may have thought.

I'd expected too that Claudine would be more reserved than she was. The two of them hit it off so well that we talked her into coming with us when we drove north to a beach so remote we had to drive twenty minutes to find a shop. A long beach with the sea breaking into surf that showed its pale force even after dark. The three of us sat on the veranda of a house we rented from a young Māori couple. We drank late and fell silent for long pauses, which seemed so natural a part of our being together, and watched the pinpoint brightness of satellites swing in their arcs above us. Jean-Paul quoted from a

French poem about the stars, and Claudine, who didn't understand the words, asked him to say the lines again.

A month that passed too quickly. I was pleased too—more than I should have been—that he didn't find us provincial. I mentioned that to Claudine, which was careless of me, but she seemed not to mind. She said, laughing, putting me in my place, 'I suppose if you come from as big a place as he does you're too sophisticated to be snobbish.' And I did my best not to be small-minded, not to notice, even when I felt it in the air—that if it were not for me, she and Jean-Paul may have liked each other more.

I would lie awake at night thinking about it. Not even appalled, as I almost certainly would have been, had she been my friend rather than my sister. I suppose I thought I knew them both too well for anything bad to come of it. Another person, perhaps, might think there was a touch of carelessness about me; or if not that, a bizarre innocence. To think differently about a thing to how almost anyone else might. My believing, as a child might, that because we were all so nice, no one would be mean. I was right about that too. Right in a way that showed how wrong I was.

I would lie and hear Jean-Paul's breathing beside me, his turning—or so I told myself—more than usual, his body telling what was on his mind. These old clichés again! All those novels I had read about real or soon-to-be real unfaithfulness, how beside the point they were when the chips were down. Did Ian McEwan, did Ali Smith, did whoever you want to throw into the mix, ever offer a shred of useful wisdom when it was needed? The inanity of literature as life instruction!

You might guess what a muddle I was in. Flattering myself for my common sense, my sad little assurance that I of all people had a discerning eye! In fact both of them, my sister and Jean-Paul, were more admirable than I. Their admitting they were in what even my mother would have called a 'moral fix'.

And now, only a year later, Claudine gone, because she chose to. Jean-Paul left, as he had always intended, to take a gallery job in Papeete.

Distraught. That word I keep writing in letter after letter, writing it in shame. But even I am not such a bitch to speak the truth about the dead. Nor do I write 'free', which reflects so badly.

REBECCA BALL

Whose Hearts the Size of Plums?

She holds each half in a red-stained palm, twists till she hears the tear of flesh from bone, lays them glistening on the chopping board. A pale sliver in the ooze. She digs in her fingers, feels warm flesh yield, bleed, pack in under her nails. He'll stare at the stain of it in the office tomorrow. She could take him a jar, couldn't she. She won't.

She rips out the stone like a brown tooth, tosses it into the bowl. Tang of metal on her tongue. She pulls more plums onto the crimson board; the pile in the sink shifts, settles. A warm drop on her bare toe. That *True Crime* episode she watched last night, those lined-up photos of women, those pale blinking men staring slack-mouthed into the camera. Didn't one of them eat the hearts afterwards? She pictures him wrapping one in a teatowel, aiming a thick stick, once, twice, beating it like a pāua in his suit and tie.

Tap of blade on bone. Slice, twist, pull apart. She sinks her fingertips back into wet flesh. An adult heart is about the size of a man's fist. But whose hearts the size of plums? Monkeys'? Cats'? Babies'? Her stomach twists and she's running the hot tap, squeezing dishwash, scrubbing red stains. *Forgodssake Sarah, make an effort with yourself would you?* His pale face in the fluorescent office lighting. His black socks on crimson carpet tiles. His slack-mouthed smile.

The pan of halved plums trembles on the bench. Later she will bring them to a rolling boil, turn steel pot into bubbling cauldron. Pour black hearts into hot glass. Stash them in the pantry. And when winter comes she will draw them out with a long-handled spoon, the fleshy squash of them on buttered toast.

BRETON DUKES

His Mouth *Is* His Heart

The car is on the road. Then it isn't. And the energy within the skid flips the vehicle mid-air, landing it roof first in the harbour.

Air leaves noisily and already the car's ceiling is a puddle. Upside down, Ian watches his wallet float past.

'George?'

Ian looks. On the diagonal, also hanging like a bat, George is in his booster seat. The other car seats are empty. Today Michelle has the younger two.

Now the car is a well-drawn bath. Reaching to unclick his own belt, Ian makes the huffing sound rugby players make just before the whistle. The belt releases. He slips into the cold. Twisting, he rights himself.

'Dad?' goes George.

Cold around his groin, Ian pisses as he pushes between the front seats. The car's no longer sinking, but water's still coming. Ian goes to unclick George's belt, but with everything inverse he reaches to the wrong side of the seat. And the water … it's in George's eyes.

It's not that Ian's heart's in his mouth, it's that his mouth *is* his heart.

'George.'

Ian has his hand in the right area, but the other kids' seats are packed tight. It's hard enough to find the buckle when the car's the right way up. And now George starts thrashing.

'Breathe, mate,' says Ian, groping between the car seats with one hand while trying to control George's head with the other.

George bucks and the car seats shift, snaring Ian's hand. Ian wrenches, but he's stuck and no matter how he holds George's head it's under water. Can he breathe into George? Hasn't he seen that on TV?

The latest argument he and Michelle have been having is around cosmetic surgery. Post babies, she wants a tighter tummy and something done to her breasts. In response he's threatening to get his hair replaced. Leaving that morning, he'd said in a hard voice, 'The kids won't recognise us, is that we want?'

It's quiet in the car. The air is gone. All except what's in Ian's lungs. Out the rear window a black shag beats past as Ian breathes into George. Past the soft, anemone feel of George's lips. And with one hand on his oldest son's neck and the other still struggling with the seat belt, George becomes a musical instrument Ian's playing.

But really, what's most true about all this is that neither of them is dead yet.

JENNY POWELL

Ngaro Huruhuru/Native Bees

Such rapid adult flight

as if the larval merging of ganglia was shaken, as if a rampage
of weather flooded sensory development, as if prenatal neglect
reduced systemic regulation, as if the rumble of urban encroachment negated
potential for sound, as if chemical insecticides decreased venomous drive

        as if such rapid adult flight was unexpected.

Hoiho

Tapping my shoulder
with your beak
on the fence.

In the space
between slats
you offer the universe
of your eye.

MADELEINE FENN

No Hands

Take my hand. There are two of us in this cave.
    —Lisel Mueller, 'The Blind Leading the Blind'

I.
Take my hand.
First love—
Look, it's so easy.

But when we walk together we do not hold hands, not in the daylight, unless in the slim intervals dictated by shadow. Lust has made us vampires. We draw no courage from each other's grip, so polluted now by the new red-handed bloom of sex on our fifteen-year-old fingers:
These hands, nocturnal creatures.

I see no way out of this fear. That is to say, my hands are tied.

II.
The hand is the intermediary between the intimate body and the external world; a stand-in for control, agency and work. Lend a hand. Have it in hand. In my own hand.

The hand is the chronically underrated sexual agent. Only pop music does it due homage: *Hands on my body*. Touch anchors experience. Touch me, touch me not.

A woman gives her hand in marriage. Her sex, her work. Does she give it? Take my hand. Hand it over. This is the handling language of the imperative. For those martial Romans, too, marriage was *cum manu* (with hand), or *sine manu* (without hand): A woman belongs to her husband's power, or remains in her father's.

Lay your hands upon me.
That's a seduction.

Lay your hands upon me.
That's an assault.

There is only one word for hand in English and it is this harsh Germanic little thing, hand. It makes me harsh too. Barbarian.

A fist (victory or violence or both). A handshake (deal done).
In 1989 a chain of two million wove its way through the three Baltic states as an independence protest, nearly 700 kilometres, hand in hand (the heart may fail where the hand will not: it unites).

The upper hand is a way to punch down.

III.
I am visiting my first deathbed. Speech is difficult here; for the dying it is senseless and far away, for the living, too close. Touch is the language left. Into my left hand, the sinister, I take her wrinkled one (trying not to think the word *emaciated*), and squeeze.

For a moment, nothing. Then, like a sparrow's heartbeat, two small pulses. I am held.

IV.
The orator Cicero's head was put up on the rostra where he gave his speeches, as punishment or warning. This is not so notable as the fact that his right hand came too, or perhaps both. Enemies close at hand: he could reach out, touch them.
An amputation, a killing, must have once been an intimate affair.

Put your hands up!
That's a party.

Put your hands up!
That's an arrest.

Manus quoque scripsisse aliquid in Antonium exprobrantes praeciderunt:
Livy tells us here how soldiers cut off Cicero's hands for his writings criticising
Mark Antony, that great sex-addled biter of the hands that fed him.

In the theory of the body politic, the hand is nothing but force: soldiers,
knights, throttling on the orders of the king-head.

But here is a fist. Here is a reckoning written in your own hand.
Peace sign. Middle finger.

V.
Between my second love and me
times come when we walk together hand-held and think nothing of it.
The politics are: who will do the dishes?

From her flat window there is a view of Dunedin's First Church. I pretend to
prick my finger on its spire. If I fall into mythic sleep, she will wake me.

She is holding my hand now as we walk together, two happy amnesiacs,
towards the door of my new home. She will only let go at the last possible minute.
This is why I love her.

This empty-handedness could frighten me if I let it. Some things cannot be
held on to (water in the cupped palms) and some must go in and out for a time
(her hand in mine).

Hélène Cixous, Coming to Writing: *Let yourself go! Let go of everything! Lose everything!*

It is my twenty-second birthday and this is what it feels like: putting your hands
up to party and ending up with a shrug. Like, huh, I got nothing.
Like, *lose everything!* Like, *… everything remains to be sought.*

I will not get a handle! I will not get a grip!
For Cixous, to be emptyhanded is what it takes to be openhanded; to open up the space to ride and read and write. So now here I am writing my bicycle, arms flung out on either side, like, look Ma—

No hands!

TONY BEYER

Troubled Land

inarticulate country churches
and their attendant cemeteries
barely visible
since the English trees have grown
shelterbelts against wrath's
eventual tirade

a sheep with a blackbird
perched on its rump
must mean something
in colonial iconography
all dark and light
all fair or foul

ninety per cent of the view
is still sky
or not so still
now the weather torments itself
and its human adherents
authors of storms and floods

in the gumboot towns
fumbling traffic
stone war memorials
visited once a year
distil the sacred blood
spilt for just this

between droughts
rain cancels the paddocks
demolishing stock and crops
until through the unmetaphorical
disputed ground
older bones start to show

Site

when the time comes
I will cross the bridge
reflected in the lake

the one not made
of wood or stone
but of light on water

blurred on occasion
when the wind intervenes
but sharper in focus

than the other
arching overhead
which is its shadow

AIMEE-JANE ANDERSON-O'CONNOR & ELIANA GRAY

Case Notes

I woke up this morning in a pool of blood. First time this has happened in years. Thighs like a finger-paint butterfly, a Rorschach test. The light shifts. I see an irregular cycle. I see crows flying north. I see a sheep sacrificed and splayed on the altar. I see a decreased chance of fertility. A crystal ball. A cycle resetting. A coin in the air. A decreased chance of fertility. I see a body bleeding onto the bathmat. There's nothing for it but to shower.

Sometimes I'm worried menstruation is going to kill me. Like that old joke that says I don't trust anything that bleeds for a week and doesn't die. How do we talk about betrayal of the body if it feels like a constant state? Focus on the pain and it becomes worse. A sharp, pointed thing across so much. Once I kept a clot so large, so bloody, because surely something made of so much of myself must still be alive?

I find myself wanting to nurse things that are not meant for me. Hold funerals for things I never thought I'd miss. I stopped bleeding once, for a year, by accident. It was the only thing that helped me move my hand from the back of my throat. My skin peach fuzz and my chest a ribbed dinghy. Now I count until the nausea leaves with the tide. I check the shore for clues. The moon's a glass marble. The poles of the earth are shivering. The months are warm and curling. My cycle's glitching again. Nobody in my family has ever waited this long.

I think about discomfort. How I spent a year in therapy learning the exact shape of the word. A philosophical exercise contained in my body. The body I've failed to understand. The number of times a needle has gone into my skin, viscera on a platter. I've been trained into acceptance since infancy, my head split open and reformed with nineteen stitches at six months old. Most doctors don't ask for consent when they touch you.

I am a lack of agency pushing forward into the abyss. Things that should be mine in strangers' hands again and again. Concepts pressed onto my skin, needled beneath it, drawn with my blood and taken to a back room I'll never see. Regurgitated to me as strings of words, no one expecting or trying to help me to understand because I was never in control in the first place.

My voice sounds louder in these white rooms, higher and younger. I try to sound sure of myself. I am unwell, but not too unwell. I have been sad lately, but not too sad. I need help, but not that much. When I was a child we didn't have money for the doctor; I had to make sure I was really sick before we went.

You have to protect yourself from the people who are trying to help you. I cry almost every time. I think about the Hippocratic oath. A backlog of bad experiences trailing behind me through every fluorescent light, every peddling antipsychotic prescription. Presenting people with a manual on how not to fuck it up. Please don't make me weigh myself. Please, just ask me first. I'm already talking to my therapist about that, thanks.

Humans are one of the only mammals that have an external menstruation. One third of our lining is excreted, the rest reabsorbed. Menstruation can be affected by stress, diet, medication, movement, the weather. I tell the endocrinologist I'm tired. She tells me: when we are under stress our uterus creates a thinner lining. This presents as a lack of external menstruation. Makes us think nothing is happening, but it is.

There are two options for treatment. How do I explain that I don't believe her? These treatments are a hospital gown. Assembly-lined and ugly. Loose around my frame. How long does it take to start listening to yourself again? Thirty-three years and counting. Rubbing the radio dial, trying to calm the static.

The doctor always takes my blood pressure at the start of our appointment, and it's always a little high. I imagine I'm a kettle, quietly screaming on the element. I try not to overthink it. I'm a collection of tissue-thin tunnels, straining at the gush. I try not to push it higher. I apologise, like it's something I messed up, and tell her I'm sorry I'm weirdly afraid of doctors, I don't know why. She usually smiles and asks me what's wrong and I tear up a little, like I've failed by being here, by admitting to the pain, submitting to the body. I blink it back like I swear this usually doesn't happen, I'm usually quite brave. She is kind enough to look straight through me and not make a fuss. This is why I've chosen her, why I wait two weeks. She nudges the tissue box closer, makes nice, professional noises and prints me off things to read later so I don't google it by myself. We test my blood pressure again at the end of the appointment and it's always perfect, on the low end of normal.

At the clinic they draw my blood into little glass cylinders shaped like shotgun casings. I hold them and taste copper on my tongue. I am surprised by the colour of cells in the fluorescent light. I feel warmer outside my skin. I touch the glass like something sacred. The nurse and I breathe together. She panics when she can't find the vein, when it slips from the needle and shrinks back to my bone. She shakes and tries again, twice, thrice, four times. I reassure her that she can keep trying, this pain is small and practical, nothing compared with the dish-towel cramp in my gut, the hot tight of my lower back. I focus on the posters on the wall, made for children. I think about the moment when body became a dirty word. About how if I had to name all my organs and pack them in a backpack, I wouldn't be able to get them all.

I imagine my uterus pink and supple like chewing gum. Warm and muscular like steak. Thinking of myself as meat makes me feel queasy. Makes me think of butchers' aprons and fields and lambs named Daisy and Mint Sauce and Roast Dinner. I squat in the shower, reach and feel animal. Shed slivered hunks and turn the floor a weeping salmon. Sometimes they cling to the ceramic like bloodied slugs and I imagine I am a tree that has dropped them from my branches. There is a grief in losing anything. My belly aches and I cradle it in my hands, imagine a melon emptied of its pips.

Dissociation is another way of saying I'll never truly belong to myself. Like being a puppet with your strings cut, slumping around an empty stage with the lights off. I think too hard about my body and suddenly there are two or more of me overlaid onto holographic sheets. It's hard enough to concentrate on the doctor speaking without the thick, incessant buzz. How do I keep misplacing myself? Forgetting that these hands are connected to these arms are connected to this face, these thoughts, the veins you can see carrying the blood you can feel. I've wanted to run away my whole life.

I watch the monitor screen and try not to hold my breath. There is a canvas of a baby, dressed in pink daisies, lying in lush white furs. I wonder if there are babies in every room and I ask the technician if it's exciting, her job? She says it gets old, they all look the same, babies are easy to find really boring, but she pretends, of course. She scans my medical notes and asks what the differential diagnosis for this is. I tell her there are two. The treatment options for both are limited, and shit. I am trembling. I am a process of elimination. The technician is just doing her job. She glances at the screen and finds the cysts immediately. She speaks like she's hit the jackpot, oh yes, she says, so many, and not too small either. The doctor says that while this news is useful, it doesn't explain the pain.

BRETT CROSS

Raglan

the boulders, litter, the sand
clamber, track, around them

pockets, of water, grey
crabs, waddling, into holes

the ragged, patches, of land
fingered, into peninsulas, cul-de-sacs

by the harbour creeping, splintering
track, further along, the coast

black sand skirt, stretched, into water
campgrounds, multiplying, into

radios, awnings, fish and chips
search, around the boulders, each

broken slumped point, to the next
bay, that stretches, forlorn, impelled

deceived, good will hunting, for
some mussel, clam, sustenance

on the shattering, of sand
bush-dark hills, lean, over harbour

kites twist, rise, descend
sift through the pebbles, the shells

the kelp, the jellyfish, the cans
eye the sun mute, sovereign

behind a smear of grey, that wipes
over the sky, white fluff, and rain

track back, track back, track back
yesterday's, strain, brimming, skin

harbour elastic, stretched smooth
in the gospel, of the broken embankments

the matchstick model, housing, the boats
that buffet, and plunge, white caps

in a solitary, small island, harbour, marooned
in the Pacific, and dark, with repetition

ELIZABETH SMITHER

Veranda or Verandah

I love the way Jane Austen spells it
for Anne Elliot's last hours
when the 'small dark rain' was falling.

Only the little boys were left at the cottage.
The Musgroves were absent with Louisa.
Anne could pace between the splashes

and reminisce until the sound of
Lady Russell's carriage, coming out of the mist
rounded it off like the added 'h'.

HOLLY FLETCHER

Everything Could Take

you are preparing names and foods
        when the stranger just walks off into a field
                and disappears behind a cloud of willows

the cattle staring as they go
        you lay down a knife / a mouth wide open
                Here—have some tea.

One hour can feel whole, like an egg
        that fits perfectly into your mouth
                everything could take one egg to get to

but doesn't

instead you crawl across the kitchen walls
        like a nameless design / patterning over whiteware
                panting from the vestibule of your mouth

you, a big shadowy mess
        who has found the false illusion
                and tried to make it last

Divisions

She assumed he wouldn't be coming home that night. And that if caught, she would blame the cat. His bedroom door was almost closed. A slight push gave way to a flat wooden arm, beckoning a welcome to both her and Mrs Wiggles. Who quickly slinked past and into the musky muddy air. Her gloved hand felt out across the slick of the wall searching for a light. The room bursting into her vision like a hangry friend, both familiar and bothersome. But she persevered, pushed now by a sense of duty. Commitment had always been her strength. She closed the door behind her and furrowed her way inside. Like a bird in a dust bath, she clucked about the room searching for the smell.

Later that night she threw the scented sack out into the street. Keeping her fingers balanced on the front door, she had to be careful to be kept inside. The doorbell had been ringing; its stench of sound had freaked the cat. She was careful to not touch the mysterious stain that had been dwelling on the front door for weeks. As she paused between the front door and the street, a person *Oi Oi*'ed her. She took the cue and started exploring her nostrils. Her search was meticulous and deep, never ending.

VICTOR BILLOT

Higher Lands

Distance is now serious,
and the meaning of distance is serious.
Not the handful of years given the young.
But many things once possible
are now impossible.
From higher lands, the view
is only backwards.
Night gathering in silent hills.
Papers with declarations,
geographies, reaching
and groping in the ocean of time.
Others burn such or never keep.
Some walk through rooms and close doors.
In the electric light of winter
I return to open them reluctantly.
Read maps after the fact.
The bitter soft flavours of the past.

PAM MORRISON

Solum
('Soil' in Gaelic)

Leaf rot, humus, dogged roots
Grind of stones on spindle shafts
Wishing bones and crackle bones
Crumble into silence bones
Calcium as palimpsest
Stories crushed to nothing left
Black as solum, black as loam
Fecund my people,
Fecund my home.

MARK EDGECOMBE

Old West Coast Road

Across the plains, power poles queued
for ceaseless progress, for the onward march
to back where we've come from, at our approach
each letting go its freight of peak or field
to take on sky. Single file of sawn-off
crosses, seemingly tireless trail of Ts,
each trunk sheathed to ward off possums,
and at each base, a pair of dots stacked
vertically, white on black, as if each cross
must carry a colon: a this equals that, a therefore,
yet one more knot in this stringing together
of extremes. The sense that yet they bear,
in spite of all that's wireless, something worth
our while—for mile after mile after mile.

MARJORY WOODFIELD

Not Over Dinner,

I say after he's suggested we watch YouTube or listen to his favourite music as we eat but then he wants to know what we'll do instead and I say let's talk but he looks confused so we eat in silence the chicken the rice the cucumber raita then sip our water because I added two heaped teaspoons of curry paste to the Thai chicken where really one would have been enough so afterwards he lies on the couch and I stand at the kitchen sink all aproned and pink-rubber-gloved looking at the back of the couch his head at one end feet dangling over the other holding his cellphone and I know this because even though I can't see it I can hear the boom thwack splatter then he comes over and says he'll help and all I can think of is Beethoven or Fauré perhaps Mozart a gentle Kyrie or Pie Jesu but now he's talking to me saying there's a trailer out for the new Dragon Ball Super Movie you need to see this me and my mate are flying up to Auckland in January when it arrives so I stand there hands in soapy suds watch the action

ANN SHELTON

i am an old phenomenon: 2022 ongoing

1. Tied together with red thread (rowan, moon tree, mountain ash).
2. Shine even into its darkest winter (fly agaric, witch's egg, devil's egg, the holy mushroom).
3. We thank you for the gift to decide the fate of man from birth (apple).
4. The loss of the oracle (cornflower, cyanus, bluebottle, bluet, bluebow, blue cap, bachelor's buttons, hurtsickle).
5. She thinks the plants (morning glory, bindweed, hedge bindweed, convolvulus).
6. She could lie on her back and sink (ginger, imbir, Asian ginger, zingiber).
7. All the herbalists and I are root diggers (roots, root diggers, wortcunners, root men, root maids).
8. Loss paving the way for her new enclosure (larkspur, lark's claw, lark's heel, lark's toe, knight's spur, delphinium, dolphin flower).

All works are archival pigment prints on Hahnemühle Bamboo, various sizes.

Systems of belief concerning the medicinal, magical and spiritual uses of plant materials were well established in the lives of European forest, nomadic and ancient peoples. However, these beliefs were forcibly supplanted as pagan practices and displaced across Europe and other continents in the wake of Christianity and the rise of capitalism. The images in i am an old phenomenon are part of the reassemblage of fragments of this old knowledge and, in their ontology, invoke the persecution of wise women, witches and wortcunners who kept this knowledge safe but whose understanding of plants and their connection with reproduction, in particular, represented a threat to the new order. This body of work and, as part of it, Pip Adam's accompanying text, 'The Three Fates', asks that we reconsider this complex nexus of lost understanding; that we re-examine the continuing persecution of women, their gender roles and physical bodies, and honour the position they have held in this long-contested space.

—Ann Shelton

PIP ADAM

The Three Fates

1.
Not so long ago, three feet under the waters to the bow of the charter yacht *Ursitoarea*, the chief steward floated on her back—arms wide, eyes open. It was 3am and the light from the moon and the dark of the sky made the underside of the surface of the sea a shimmering screen. She'd left the bottom bunk of her cabin, stepped with hardly any weight through the crew mess, past the galley, up the stairs through the main salon and onto the swim landing. No one stirred. They all slept—she made sure of it.

'You should leave the swim landing down,' she'd whispered earlier while she and one of the deckhands were having dinner.

'Sorry,' he'd said.

'You have lovely eyes,' she'd said.

She'd slipped from the open landing into the water. She had no desire to dive. Diving was something people who didn't live on boats did. Diving was a tourist move. She was underwater now. She'd always been less buoyant than anyone she met. Just like her grandmother, just like her grandmother's grandmother. She could lie on her back and sink. She'd shown someone once and their face had gone grey, like all their blood had turned to ice. So she never showed anyone again. So she did it in the dark. Off the back of the yacht. With as little splash as possible.

And this was where she was now. Under the waters off Šibenik. Looking at the screen of the underside of the surface but mainly listening. Mainly listening to the sea rising and falling to the boat, the slap and the glug, and through it, amplified almost by the crest and the trough, the noises of the people sleeping inside the boat. The bosun and his two deckhands, one awake on watch in the bridge. Her first and second stews, both asleep now, and finally the captain.

The master bedroom was huge—for a yacht. It was gauche and gold and every morning while the guests were having breakfast, so it happened for them like magic, she or one of the other stewards would pick up their clothes, clean their bathrooms and iron the linen on their beds. The cleaning was like ritual at this point in the season. They polished the chrome like the yacht was a large, living thing. They talked to it, whispering their dreams into the showers and toilets as they cleaned up the parts of the guests that were left behind.

'There's a hair in my shower,' he'd said, and he'd stood there while she got on her knees and removed it from the stall with a piece of toilet paper.

When the stewards were alone in the cabins they carried round a spray bottle of Febreze and they would spray it, then iron the bed linen, then spray it again. Like bringing the outside down into the cabins, which were almost below the water line.

The people who came on the charter yacht were the worst kind of people. Rich enough to charter a yacht but not rich enough to own a yacht. Rich enough to purchase a serfdom but only for three days, only in the boundaries of yachts like the *Ursitoarea*.

This was a particularly bad bunch. The night before last he'd thrown a hundred-dollar bill at her. The captain had told her to cut him off because he was very drunk and he'd been terrible and then he'd thrown the note at her and shouted, 'That's to pay for my terrible behaviour.'

'I can't accept it,' she'd said as it bounced off her arm.

It was still on the floor of the salon in the morning. The second and third stew had cleaned up around it. No one wanted to touch it because they knew he'd be back for it. He knew what it meant if someone picked it up. All of them knew how that would tie them to him. Or how it would make them look like a thief.

Last night he'd tried it on with the third stew. Wanted to know who she slept with. Wanted to know if she'd sleep with him. Back in London, three days before, a teenager had had his baby. All the crew were good at it—talking to drunk, rich men—but none of them enjoyed it. It all went a bit smoother when she was the chief stew. The guests got tired faster, they decided to go to bed as if it was their own idea. They ran out of puff when they wanted to complain. They left better tips.

'I don't know what you do,' the captain had said. 'But I always want you on my boat.'

She'd smiled. She had a winning smile.

'I'd rather have you with me than against me,' he'd said. And her heart sank but only a little because he had said the nice thing first and he had no idea and she cleaned his cabin too.

'I'll do the turn-downs,' she'd said, once the third stew was safe. Once the guests were all on the aft deck looking at the city talking more shit, sneaking him drinks when they thought the stews weren't looking. The yacht was big for a yacht but it was small, the crew lived very close together but there was a corner in the engine room where there was a tarpaulin and under the tarpaulin she had hidden them. Plants and parts of plants she'd pushed into olive jars and empty tequila bottles then suspended in water then sealed again. She moved them around the boat when things got bad like this. Left them under beds, inside cupboards, to fix the men. Not to repair them—to make them stay where they were. Make the women of the yacht safe. And as she did the turn-downs, Febreze in hand, she'd hidden jars in the master stateroom, in both the twin cabins. And when she got back they were all tired.

'You should go to bed,' she said.

'We should go to bed,' he said. Squeezing her shoulder as he said it.

And now she was under the water, listening to the people, listening to the boat but ready now to speak to the plants. Suspended as they were in water, she addressed **the tree [...] with the respectful name of elder** and reminded the parts of it in the jar that she had known it for a long time, that for centuries they had called on Sundays to **sit down under the house elder when they wanted to visit with their descendants and relatives** wearing **pointed hats made of birch bark to make it clear that they weren't evil spirits**.[1] Her people had lived within its branches and when the tree bled red it was with their blood in its sap. She had never burnt an elder. Every man that came within 50 feet of her eventually said she was evil. A nasty piece of work. But surely the small white flowers in the water in the caper jar—slimy, breaking down—could see she had done the right things and would extend their help to her and the women of the boat.

She'd seen the leaves of the ginger in the groundcover of a castle where they'd set up a dinner for the guests.

'You go ahead,' she'd said to the second stew, and she'd made herself invisible and dug up the root that was now in the water in the jar from the ground. She understood that **the plant's root, which penetrates easily into the** dark depths of the earth, penetrates easily into the dark interior of the body and with its strength can drive out the 'worms' and render them harmless.[2] Her grandmother had told her. And she hadn't taken all of it. She told the root now, she had only taken what she needed and it hummed back at her smoky pink like a toe and as he slept, in the golden cabin, it drove out the worm.

And as she said thanks and spoke spells, something made itself out on the underside of the surface of the sea, and she found herself saying, 'Once upon a time, beside one of the long tables in the restaurant Soarta a man was shouting at my sister-waitress.' And she reached out to pull her under, to take her away from the shouting man.

2.
The restaurant was deep and dark, lit in a way that made you feel like there was actually nothing there. There was a sense of the walls disappearing into the air and of the outside coming in. They served things ground to soil, and roots and lichen still on branches, and tonight they were serving Fly Agaric for Christmas.

The waitress felt wet, all at once and all over her, soaked through and floating but she was dry and at a table and the man was talking to her, shouting at her, not to be heard over the Christmas crowd but still loudly because he was right and she was wrong. She was listening, actively, nodding, agreeing that she was wrong and then all of sudden she was wet, or she felt wet, the swish of something past her face, a leaf from the land slimy with being under water for too long.

Soarta specialised in foraged wild food, so maybe she had somehow inhaled something hallucinogenic. She put her hand to her eyes to sweep the water away but her skin was dry in the restaurant heating. He was still shouting. Surely they didn't mean Fly Agaric because you can't eat Fly Agaric—even as a child he knew that and he pointed at the menu, at the picture of the five red-and-white toadstool fungi. He had paid a lot to be at the restaurant—everyone had. He had paid for all these people too, he explained, waving a hand over the long table at his employees. He thought it was the best but a mistake like this showed he was better.

What seemed most important was that everyone knew that—that he was the best, that he knew more than the world-renowned chef. Maybe, in the end, this would make the expense worth it. This scene, she thought, is what he pays for. And now she had to explain without making it necessary for him to lose this. He was a baby. He had been a baby and maybe she had been at his christening, but he was being a baby now.

So she nodded and let him talk to give herself time. He was wrong of course, because of course you could eat them.

'Without hallucinogenic effect?' he said and she realised she'd said it out loud so there was nothing left to do but nod and say, 'With special handling.' And he was silent, finally, and she filled the space with, 'If they are boiled in large amounts of water for a lengthy time and then drained and re-boiled and drained and re-boiled you can eat them. The Russians have always eaten them. It requires incredible skill.'

He was looking at her now and it was awkward so she said, 'So,' and ran through the drinks order.

It was a tasting menu. A nightmare, and when finally the Fly Agaric arrived, she stood at the head of the table next to him and said, '**The lovely, red Fly Agaric (*Amanita muscaria*) lives in symbiosis with birch and spruce. People have used this circumpolar mushroom to communicate with dwarves, gods, and ancestors in Eurasia as well as in North America since at least the Upper Paleolithic period, especially during the dark nights of the winter solstice time. The fungus seems to shine the sunlight caught by the birch directly into the depths of the soul, even into its darkest corners.**'[3]

And in the end, he applauded the Fly Agaric with everyone else and the chef came out and the music was stopped and everyone turned to the chef and he told the story of Christmas and the toadstool. '**Santa**,' he said, '**is a modern counterpart of a shaman, who consumed mind-altering plants and fungi to commune with the spirit world [...] as the story goes, up until a few hundred years ago these practicing shamans or priests connected to the older traditions would collect *Amanita muscaria* (the Holy Mushroom), dry them, and then give them as gifts on the winter solstice [...]**

***Amanita muscaria* is found throughout the Northern Hemisphere under conifers and birch trees, just like presents found under the Christmas tree by excited and happy children. This explains the tradition of the Christmas tree and the gifts, wrapped in red and white, placed under the tree just like the magic mushrooms.**

***Amanita muscaria* is classified as poisonous, this might be a reason the**

shamans of that time initially hang the fresh Amanita muscaria to dry on tree branches, just like the colourful ornaments on a Christmas tree.

Santa's flying reindeer have a similar connection to the *Amanita muscaria* mushrooms. Reindeer, in general, are common across Europe and Siberia, and just like the human inhabitants of these areas, they too consumed mushrooms. Harvard University biologist Donald Pfister suggests that Siberians who ingested the mushrooms may have hallucinated that the grazing reindeer were actually flying.'[4]

With the darkness of the room and the chef's sonorous and practised telling of the story and the amount of food everyone had eaten, and the warmth of the heat and perhaps the toadstool itself (because maybe she had taken the water the agaric had been cooked in and only disposed of most of it when she had been asked to dispose of all of it and maybe she had put one drop of it in each drink she served—maybe more than a drop in his drink), everyone in the room swam a little and the walls and roof pulled back to Paleolithic times and the horizon spread out like a workbench and was sparkling and everyone looked up and into this ancient place an airplane rose into the sky, slowly, slipstreams behind it and the waitress said, 'Once, there was a private jet called *Moartea* and in it a man is preying on my sister-steward.'

3.
The air steward felt warm all of a sudden, an outside cold, inside warm warmth. All over and all at once. He had called the plane *Moartea* because he thought it meant something else. He was leaning on her and maybe it was his leaning that was making her hot. He ran hot. He'd told her before. It was his plane so she worked for him. She was beautiful, he said, and he leaned in even closer and touched her hair. Then his wife came out of the bathroom and he pulled back and the steward felt better but still hot, so it wasn't him after all.

'The arrangement,' his wife said, and she pointed at it, and the steward nodded. 'Are these cornflowers?'

'I'm not sure,' said the steward.

'They look cheap,' she said. 'Can you get rid of them?'

'She can't get rid of them,' he said, laughing at his wife. 'We're three thousand feet in the air.'

'Put them somewhere I can't see them,' she said, and she adjusted her suit jacket—the baby would come in three days—and she sat down and looked at her phone.

'Of course,' the steward said. 'Of course.'

The arrangement was huge, wired into a trunk. It had arrived that morning. His wife had asked for rustic but it wasn't what she wanted. She meant peonies, or rosehips. This was huge and sparse and didn't smell of anything but the forest.

The steward started delicately to reach in for the cornflowers. She knew they were cornflowers, she'd said she wasn't sure so his wife could feel smart, it helped but the steward knew they were cornflowers. And she knew that cornflowers could be **filtered through three layers of blue linen and then ritually consecrated beneath the full Moon with a moonstone; she knew that then the linen may be used to bathe the eyes, bringing an increased sense of clairvoyance, enabling one to see aspects of the creative forces of the Universe.**[5] As she pulled them out she thanked them, gently crushing their petals, carefully, not enough to attract him but just enough so she could see them landing safely.

They were fighting now. Quietly needling at each other, although he was getting louder. There were sloe berries in the arrangement, a divining rod, she thought as she ran her hands over it, trying to look like she was busy with the arrangement and somehow invisible and somehow not less than three feet from the fight. A wishing rod. Then she just started listing them to try to drown out the terrible things they were saying to each other. Hawthorn, achillea, sloe, morning glory, elder, feverfew, cornflower, birch, apple—birch. **With a broom made of birch twigs, one sweeps rooms and sacred places; during the Alemannic carnival, the archaic, colourful festival at which many costumed and masked people parade as various 'spirits' in February, the witches still carry a birch broom, occasionally 'riding' it and symbolically swooshing it around to cleanse the atmosphere.**[6] She lifted the birch branch out of the arrangement and swung it slightly; the plane lurched in the direction of her sweep. She swung it the other way and the plane lurched that way. She flung it up, then down. They were silent now. She drew a zigzag with it and the plane thumped up and down.

'Sister-steward,' she whispered. 'Sister-waitress.'

And Soarta replied, 'Moartea?' and she replied, 'Yes.' And they both said,

'Ursitoarea?' and from under the water in the Croatian Sea Ursitoarea replied, 'Yes.'

And together, from across thousands of miles and at the same time so close they were touching, they say, in the ritual to recognise the immediacy of the threat, '**The rotten face of a corpse floating among the rushes and the plastic bags swept in from the road on the breeze, dark mask seething under a myriad of black snakes smiling.**'[7] The slain are with us and we are with the slain, the grandchildren of the witches they couldn't kill standing in the responsibility that comes with the power to decide the fate of man.'

---

1   Wolf D. Storl, *The Untold History of Healing: Plant lore and medicinal magic from the Stone Age to present* (North Atlantic Books, 2017), pp. 180–81.
2   Ibid., p. 170.
3   Ibid., pp. 72–74.
4   Mustafa Itani, 'Santa and magic mushrooms: The Shamanic origins of Christmas traditions', *Medium*, 2 December 2018.
5   Paul Beyerl, *A Compendium of Herbal Magick* (Phoenix Publishing, 1998), p. 140.
6   Storl, *The Untold History of Healing*, p. 70.
7   Fernanda Melchor, *Hurricane Season*, translated by Sophie Hughes (Text Publishing Company, 2020), p. 13.

Ann Shelton has commissioned several short stories by Pip Adam for use within her artworks and books. Shelton provides Adam with access to her research materials and with key reference points that are critical to the conceptual basis for Shelton's artwork. Here, Shelton shared her interest in the submerged, or, the water-bound: the literal reference of witches' brews, tinctures and tea; the sublimated pedagogy of plant lore; and the practice of 'swimming the witch', the tying up and dunking of the accused into a body of water to determine if they are innocent or guilty—if they sink or float. The quotations encased in the story are excerpts from Shelton's research materials.

PIP ROBERTSON

The Previous Assistant

Another standing ovation. Molloy was centre stage, tears in his eyes, hands limp at his sides, while the audience clapped. Jess watched from the back of the auditorium, the applause travelling up her spine. All my words, she thought.

They met in Molloy's suite after the formal dinner. The new assistant called the speech genius and tried to show Molloy the online reaction, but he waved him away. The assistant turned to Jess, but she didn't care now the speech was done. She needed to focus on the next one.

'You want to make yourself useful?' Molloy said to the assistant. 'Call room service. Get me a burger.'

He nodded, practically bowed. Another acolyte, Jess thought. So eager to be here, fighting the good fight. The previous assistant had called it her life's honour to work for Molloy. Who even talks like that? Jess never had liked her.

'Look at this,' Molloy said. He reached into his pocket and handed Jess a rosebud, white petals tipped pink.

'It's a radish, from dinner,' Molloy said. 'The main course looked like a fucking corsage. I didn't know whether to eat it or pin it to my chest and wait to be asked to dance.'

He shook his head at the artistry, or maybe the artifice. Molloy read meaning into food. One trip they were welcomed at the airport with a military brass band and state photographers. But Molloy had returned from lunch with a cloth napkin in his pocket.

'Camel tongue,' he had said, unwrapping an oily disc of meat. 'They knew we'd find it repulsive. We may as well fuck off now—they're going to concede nothing.'

Blisters were forming on Jess's feet. She pictured the slippers in her room: plush and white in their plastic wrap.

'Do we have the final wording yet?' she asked the assistant.

The finer details of a partnership were being worked through. Jess had written as much as she could of the following morning's announcement speech, but needed the final text of the agreement to finish it. There were sticking points around the environmental measures Molloy insisted on.

The assistant checked his phone. 'Not yet, sorry.'

'Why are you sorry?' Molloy said. 'Is it your fault?'

The assistant laughed, apologising for the apology, but Jess saw his jaw was clenched as he turned away. She didn't know how much he knew. He was hired quickly.

Molloy nodded at her. 'Go, relax. He'll call when I need you.'

Before Molloy, Jess worked in a bar. She had a useless grad degree and a prizewinning book of poems called *Smile, and Other Advice*. The central sequence was crafted from comments she had received from men. It came out right when people were adding #MeToo to all their social posts, and making jokes about men's splayed legs on public transport. It rode a wave of popularity—insofar as books of poems ever rode waves—and won a national award.

Capturing the zeitgeist had been inadvertent. Jess didn't know what to write next. She sat at her computer every afternoon, mind blank, waiting for the time she had to leave for her shift. She resisted social media and played solitaire instead. It seemed a nobler form of procrastination. When she did well the pack of cards leapt about the screen to congratulate her. No poem had ever done that. Not even the ones that won the prize.

She knew of Molloy before working for him—everyone did. He used to be famous not for anything he had achieved—something to do with property and offshore investments—but for the wealth he had amassed. He was married, for a while, to a celebrity chef, and implicated in the breakup of a cricketer and soap star. The shift to philanthropy was abrupt. He had always been described as a self-made man, but when he launched the foundation he spoke publicly for the first time about his childhood. The grim timeline of violence and neglect seemed barely believable, but journalists verified it with court reports and old news items.

Jess had started out drafting replies to requests Molloy received for interviews and appearances at events. They were logged in a spreadsheet and Jess was responsible for the ones with a No next to them. She wrote personalised variations on Mr Molloy regretfully declines. Someone else did the 'warmly accepts'. She saw Molloy sometimes in the hallway but never spoke to him. The atmosphere was different when he was in the office. Everyone was aware and adjusted a little, like flowers subtly tilting their faces towards the sun.

Jess had been regretfully declining for three months when the speech request came in. She worked late to make the three-hour deadline, emailed it back, and heard nothing more. The following week she gathered with colleagues to watch the livestream.

'Don't be disappointed,' said the main speechwriter Gavin, a nervy ex-crime reporter, as Molloy came on stage. 'He always rewords.'

But as Molloy spoke, it was like hearing someone call lottery numbers that matched her ticket.

'Did you write that bit?' someone asked her, as Molloy paused for a burst of applause.

'I wrote it all so far.'

'All of it?'

'Yeah. Word for word.'

Gavin stalked off and the person next to Jess elbowed her in the side.

'Congrats on the new job.'

'I don't think it means that.'

'Uh, yeah, it does. Everyone knows he's been looking to replace Gavin.'

Molloy told her once that the worst mistake a person could make was to surround himself with people who think like him.

'That's why I need you,' he had said.

Jess's room was at the back of the same hotel. It looked out on a concrete wall and electric cables like jungle vines. She kicked off her shoes and inspected the damage: one heel rubbed raw, the other on its way. New shoes on a trip was a rookie mistake and she should have known better. She slid into the hotel slippers. The first trips she always took the slippers home—hotels throw them away after each guest anyway. But they never felt as comfortable at home.

She looked through the bathroom for something to help the blisters. Nothing. All the little bottles and packages. What was that scent—lychee, grapefruit? She didn't bother taking them home anymore either.

That morning she had been in Molloy's car from the airport to run through the day's speech. It was the scenic route, down state-of-the-art motorways, avoiding the blue tarpaulin settlements. Molloy had been reading the notes aloud when his phone rang.

'Alec,' he said. 'Update me.'

Alec, his lawyer. Also his friend.

'Cannot happen,' Molloy said. 'Do you hear me? Make her stop.'

He'd hung up and leaned back against the headrest.

'That stupid girl,' he had said. 'If she isn't careful she's going to wreck everything.'

Jess had looked out the window. They were on a colonial avenue by then. Buildings ornate as wedding cakes. She didn't need to be told who he was talking about.

If asked, Jess could honestly say she hadn't had much to do with the previous assistant. Day-to-day emails, a few meetings through the week. It wasn't like they were friends. Jess wasn't her confidante. First Jess knew she'd left was when she emailed her and got an auto-reply saying she no longer worked there.

Molloy always called the assistant 'girl'. Ask the girl. Get the girl to do it. He used the same arch tone when he called Jess 'our poet', or Anton in the marketing team 'the yeti'. He had pushed the assistant hard. Long hours, exacting tasks. But Molloy pushed everyone hard.

The hotel window opened only wrist wide. The night air was warm and thick, like dipping her hand into soup. In the dark alley below she could just make out someone curled up asleep in the shadows near an overflowing rubbish skip. Rats moved about their feet. She willed the sleeper to wake but they kept lying there. No point calling reception—someone would take out another bag of rubbish soon enough, and hotel security would force them to leave. The police would likely do worse.

Her phone pinged. She hoped it was the final wording for her, but no.

Hey love, how's it going? Rob, up early.

Usual circus xx, she wrote.

No need to say she was still working. It was a sore point: Rob thought the job was too punishing, even though he was the one who had suggested she apply. Maybe it would even help her poetry, he had said, like it was a chronic condition.

Jess realised she had nodded off when her phone hummed against her neck on the pillow.

'Done,' the assistant said. 'I'm emailing you the final version. Molloy needs the speech finished, like, now.' Not so chirpy when the boss isn't around, Jess noted.

Jess filled in the gaps in the speech, adjusted the opening and the end, and sent it. She washed her face, put on lipstick and the painful shoes.

Back in his suite, Molloy paced, reading the speech aloud to commit it to memory—he never used notes on stage. Jess prompted him when he faltered. The assistant listened in, planning the 10-second soundbites for social. Once Molloy mostly had the speech, he and Jess practised for the panel discussion that would follow it.

'The citizens—'

'Communities, not citizens,' Jess said.

'Girls and boys around the world deserve—'

'Children. It's better, non-binary.'

'Climate change—'

'Crisis, not change. Always, always, climate crisis.'

When the assistant was distracted she asked Molloy, 'Any word? On the other thing, from the car.'

'Nothing,' he said. 'Nothing and so we go on.'

If anyone asked Jess later whether she saw anything, she didn't have much to tell.

There was the conference on the island, where Molloy was keynote speaker. The assistant hadn't been around most of the day, blaming food poisoning. But that evening she was at the bar with everyone, pale and tense, sipping soda water.

'This isn't compulsory, you know. You can leave,' Jess had said. The assistant had looked to Molloy as if for permission, but he was talking to someone else. She was still there when Jess left to go to bed.

Sometimes Jess knocked on Molloy's door, and he said to come in, but when he saw her he said, 'Oh, it's you,' neither pleased nor displeased, but like he was rearranging his face, his manner, and it was obvious he had been expecting someone and something else.

And there was one time in the bathroom at work. It was late, hardly anyone about, and the assistant mustn't have known Jess was in the stall. Jess came out to find her at the basin, crying, doing something with a paper towel up her skirt. She dropped the skirt, scrunched the towel in her hand, wouldn't meet Jess's eyes in the mirror.

'Everything okay?'

'Fine,' she had snapped.

Jess didn't see her again after that.

Jess was sleeping when Molloy called. She sat up.

'It's confirmed,' he said. 'The girl's pressing charges. The whole lot. We're leaving early, so be ready straight after the speech.'

'Okay.'

'I've been warned that police will be meeting the plane. Beyond that, I don't know, but there'll no doubt be media, cameras. And they know you, so—'

'So I need to be prepared. I assumed as much.'

'You'll be all right?'

'I'll have to be.'

'And for work, I mean? My engagements will be cancelled for the foreseeable, and I'll understand if you choose to move on.'

'I'll find something.'

He sighed. 'What the fuck am I going to say?'

Jess hung up. He was on his own for that.

If anyone asked Jess, what about you, did he ever …?, she could honestly say never. That wasn't defending him. It didn't mean anything. The remarkable thing, Jess thought, was not that men like Molloy kept doing it, but that anyone ever thought they would stop.

She got out of bed, opened the curtains. Dawn. The sky would have been pink if it weren't for the pollution. She should call Rob to tell him. Looking down, she could see now that it hadn't been a person sleeping in the alley at all, but bags of rubbish. Rats or dogs had strewn the contents everywhere. Her bleeding heels had left marks like kisses on the sheets. The radish rose was on the windowsill, wilting just like a real one.

Should she try to find meaning in these things? Wasn't that what a poet would do?

She called Molloy back. He answered on the first ring.

'Woman, not girl,' she said. 'When you talk about her, never call her girl.'

PHOEBE WRIGHT

Actual Forever

I dream that the angel of death turns out to be the
Briscoes lady, after codeine and too much wine,
two nights before you die.

The doctor has assisted eight deaths since the law changed: The
greatest prevention of suffering in his career.
But an unbidden, unvoted-for voice in my head says,
Murderer. Says, *Leave this house.*

Many books claim to be about death, but they are really
about life: How to prepare, grieve, and talk to the children.
Not about actual forever death.

If anyone describes what happens after with too much conviction,
we think they are crazy.
We think this quietly if they are religious and we are
respectful. But we still think it.

I borrow one of your jackets, and there's a damp hanky in the
pocket. I think, *ew, gross, a future dead woman's hanky.*
I realise I am also a future dead person.

As we wait for the doctor, as you carefully put your necklace in an
envelope, as you don't change your mind, a voice in my head,
unwanted, unedited, *rhyming*, sings a nursery song
for future generations:

We are sitting drinking tea,
Till the doctor comes to set you free.

Ghosting means the opposite of what it normally means if it's
a dead person doing it.
You said you'd ghost me if you could.

We put your ashes in an almost spherical dark-glazed
casserole pot from the op shop. I feel a confusing,
adjacent-culture twinge about tikanga.
Urns are exploitatively expensive.

Now I'm in a car in the rain, and this would be a good time to
ghost me if you can. But you are not here.
Only your ball of ashes, weighing in my lap
like the mother of all full stops.

DANNY BULTITUDE

Sons of God

First time I'd ever been on a boat
Ashtrays said 'leave butts here' so we sat on them
Old disposable camera days of not knowing
What the light would capture

Teachers assured us the title of
Christian Camp was nothing to fear
Yet we sat through renditions of 'Jesus Was a Cool Dude'
And couldn't eat dinner unless we sang along

I stood aside with the three Hindu kids
When the staff asked 'Who wants to feel Jesus's pain?'
And passed around a yellow onion
Expecting us to bite into it like an apple

Evangelical Josh wanted to, hand waving wildly
Near jumping from his seat for the opportunity
And we all admired the hole made by his one big munch
As we passed the onion to the person beside us

Nobody else bit, instead feeling the holy pain
Of teachers noticing our morning boners when they woke us
Of toothpaste squirted between pillow and pillowcase
Of cold tunafish sandwiches on paper plates

But moreso than any onion was the kid
Who slid down the metal waterslide before the water was on
To impress some of the girls
But got his arms caught and broke the bones inside

Took the ambulance two long hours to show
And he lay there crying with both broken arms spread wide
But nobody, not even the devout staff,
Recognised the parallel.

MEGAN KITCHING

Mātātā | Fernbird

There is a point beyond which everything frays.
I keep what's left of me below that brim
brightly busy with my lot of straws.
A little wind makes it down here,
just a broom-brushing, an up-gust
or two of greenward light moves
the tawny rattan interior where I was born,
not so much hatched as thatched,
made for this humble life of weaving around stems.

I don't have faith in a higher place.
Look at the summits, stoned cold and loveless.
You couldn't hear yourself call up there.
The exposure above all: three-sixty air
unseaming feathers, knocking you claws over beak
scrambling for a prop, horrified by distance
so only a thin whistle-moan comes out.
That's the pining sound the stars make.
They put their heads up proud as flowers
but wagged too long and the wind rose,
blew their tops off far into the night.

I believe in recurrence. The world
when you get down to it is tiled like my tail
of tufts, tessellated tussock, hebe, flax
in a scribble of resemblance going around—
I don't mean the blur from the clouds,
that appalling loss of horizon—just
climbing out twig height to discern

that you aren't alone, that the plucky pith
of grass knits this hill into hills.
That's why I perch and speak: snip snip
snip like ripe pods snapping,
loosing grains of voice to commute and meet
the echoes of another seeding the breeze
with repetition and so we go on,
far beneath the gods working at the pattern.

KIRSTIE McKINNON

Glennie

I go to see you in the hospital room
you have smallened, your face smooth planed
we listen to Beethoven, you recognise the sonata
but cannot tell me what it is, I chatter through
obvious pain, hold your hand.
Outside on Frederick Street a child in a pram
holds a dry plane tree leaf forward like a sword.
I pick up a fallen leaf too, as if I can still play.
I look up at your window, the eighth floor
with last light glancing towards Mt Cargill.

REBECCA READER

What the Universe Can Do for You

If Janine weren't a yoga teacher with a studio two floors above a donut outlet, Bruce would say she was a professional megalomaniac. When the yogis bring their hands to their hearts to set an intention, she says, 'Ask yourself what the universe can do for you.' She doesn't consider herself to be the random fallout of a zillion chemical reactions, a waste product that grew one too many neurons and invented novelty socks and labradoodles. She doesn't see that the art of survival lies in embracing personal pointlessness. Every time she says, 'Make the universe work for you,' Bruce waits until she has turned the heater off and is heading for the door so that he can say, 'Now here's the thing.' Bruce has never said this. It has been four years and five days since Bruce started Power Up classes with Janine.

Janine has the marble musculature and smouldering detachment of a Greek statue behind alarmed glass. She could pick up a hefty guy like Bruce, throw him out the window, fix her hair, then head into town to buy chickpeas. But this is all hypothetical because, sadly, everything about Bruce and Janine is hypothetical. Tonight, he's in pigeon pose when Janine says, 'The universe isn't for cowards.' And yet there he is, face down, a shin under his chest, his forearms on the ground, surrendering, like the world has him at gunpoint, like a guy with only ten seconds to say, 'Now here's the thing.' Class ends. He slides his yoga blocks into his bag as the last student leaves. Then he says, 'Now here's ...' just as Janine walks over to the mat cupboard and karates it shut with her naked foot. 'Anything I can help you with, Bruce?' she says, but he's already out of the door and halfway down the stairs to Party Palace Donuts.

Party Palace Donuts is on the ground floor of Giacomo's Mini Mall, a building that used to be Casanova's Nightclub cum strip bar. On the pavement outside are two advertising boards, one for Pacific Power Yoga, and the other for Party Palace Donuts, and because of all the Ps, people get them confused. They go through the door to Pacific Power for a cinnamon twist, and they go to Party Palace to seek truth in the moment. Or maybe, like Bruce, they can't always tell the good from the bad, the heaven from the hell.

Bruce likes the polished oak floorboards of Pacific Power, but sometimes he craves sticky lino beneath his feet. That's just him. Some people never go to Pacific Power. They only go to Party Palace. They are truly damned, according to the yoga-nut religion. Some go to Pacific Power but never to Party Palace. They are truly blessed, according to the yoga-nut religion but truly damned by everyone outside it. Bruce likes to be neither damned nor saved. It's the safest way. Find a fence. Don't sit on it. Look for the gate. Get the best of both paddocks.

Bruce has just ordered a box of Boston Cremes when Janine walks in. He has never seen her this side of the fence before. She looks up at the food screens and sucks her lips in at the side like, if she's not careful, she'll be tube-fed twenty Caramel Munchkins. He's tempted to recommend a ring donut because the ring donut embodies what he thinks about Janine's approach to the universe. All those sprinkles, all that glaze and deep-fried dough orbit around—you guessed it—nothing. They aren't hanging around to do the hole the favour. They're getting on with life being crunchy and calorific. Janine buys a bottle of water and waves it at him on the way out. He waves a bitten Boston Creme. Same move, different languages.

The box keeps Bruce company all night. They watch ten episodes of a cop drama set in a mining town with smutty weather and a resident cannibal who drives a courier van and wraps body parts in bubble wrap to keep his chiller draw clean. Psychopaths make Bruce feel a whole lot more positive about his life above High and Dry Cleaners. His flat is ten metres square. The shower is in the kitchen and the dining table is in the hallway. The flat is so small that even the fixtures and fittings are trying to find somewhere else to go. His ex-wife comes round once a week with their two kids who also won't fit in the flat. So he takes them to the swings across the road, where the neighbourhood Alsatian, Sweetheart, keeps the local plastic surgeon in business. If Bruce thought too hard about his life, the smallness of it, he'd staple rump steak to his tracksuit and head for the park. So he doesn't. He reaches out for the final donut and sees what it has to offer him.

One donut has around thirty grams of sugar and a quarter of the total daily calorie requirement for an adult male. Bruce searched this up yesterday, when

Party Palace dropped a ton of flyers around town claiming that 'donuts set you free' and 'donuts promote progress'. The flyer has a picture of a skydiver in a Party Palace T-shirt about to fling himself from a cargo-hold and head for the ground at a freaky number of miles an hour. It turns out that Bruce is far more of a sucker for crafty advertising than he is for self-discipline, or anything else the universe might have to offer him. While the cannibal is filleting one of the cops, he finishes off the donut. Freedom means choice, and progress is mostly a matter of opinion.

By 3am, every episode has played out and the cat is licking the empty box. The cat doesn't give a furball about the universe. Like Bruce, it's just staying alive on sugar and monosodium glutamate. Three years ago it dragged its skin and bones through a gap in Bruce's bathroom window and ate half a tube of toothpaste. After that it just kept coming around, licking his empty food boxes, until one day Bruce christened it Dunker because it always smelt of fried food. Dunker comes inside at 6pm on the dot because that's when Bruce makes himself feel better by watching the world fall apart on the news and sometimes forgets to eat the last chicken wing.

Bruce and Dunker share the same fundamental belief that the cosmos is no gift horse, that the best things in life are right in front of you rather than overhead. Dunker only looks up when Sweetheart muscles into the yard behind the dry cleaner's and the top of the fence has the sudden appearance of salvation. Bruce looks up only when he's checking out the food screens in Party Palace. It's enough trying to keep himself alive with everything Earth throws at him without fretting over rogue asteroids, aliens, solar flares.

He has this friend, Astro Joe, who stares at the sky so much that the back of his neck is shorter than the front. Astro Joe can't drop his chin to his chest anymore, which means he's so lost in cosmic theories he's blind to the joys of Earth. He's a masochist, addicted to the flavour of his own insignificance. So whenever he goes with Bruce to Party Palace, he orders the Russian Roulette of mini donuts where one of them tastes of barf. Bruce doesn't know how Astro Joe lives that way. Astro Joe doesn't even have the comfort of a cat with a similar approach to life. At night, Dunker sleeps with his tail across Bruce's neck, so no matter how bad Bruce's days get, he always starts them glamorous as a gangster's moll.

A week after Janine's bare foot kicked the mat door shut, Bruce rolls out of bed smooth as Mrs Al Capone and by evening he's desolation in a tracksuit, standing outside Giacomo's Mini Mall with a polar wind root-canalling his molars. The choice is happy hour donuts at Party Palace or self-belief at Pacific Power, but the decision has assumed colossal importance and glued him to the pavement. It's like he's finally being forced to decide between the blameless life of colonic irrigation and kombucha, and the debauched life of acid reflux and Coke floats. The kombucha or the floats? The floats or the kombucha?

Then Janine turns up like an answer to life's eternal question, in a poncho and a pompom hat. She's carrying Party Palace water again, and Bruce has no idea where he gets the courage from, but he says, 'How do you buy the water, Janine, but never the donuts?'

'Resisting temptation isn't so hard,' she says. 'It's knowing what's worth resisting that's the problem. If it makes you happy, why resist it?'

'A Boston Creme contains a whole ton of happiness,' says Bruce. 'Not to mention freedom and progress.'

Janine glances at the Party Palace sign, her head to one side, as if she's been coming at donuts from the wrong angle her entire life.

'Hard to believe a donut can do that for a person, eh?' says Bruce.

She blinks a few times, chewing the idea over. Then she says, 'I believe it, but eggs don't always agree with me. I come out in hives that lower my vibrations.'

'The universe is full of vibrations, according to my pal Astro Joe. Tons of strings vibrating all over the place.'

'There you go,' she says. 'I need to hang on to whatever the universe has given me. But sometimes …' She opens her bag and shows him one Caramel Munchkin in greaseproof paper that she says makes her a bona fide living-and-breathing human being.

'Breathing, but for how long, if the eggs … you know,' says Bruce. Then he can't help himself. The words just come bundling out. 'Hives, eh? You know what they say. Men don't make eyes at girls with hives.'

She steps backwards and almost loses her balance on a tree root cracking up the pavement. But Bruce doesn't get to save her. He doesn't even get to say sorry because she bolts up the steps to the studio, knocking into a potted sage and making it rock in its saucer.

Maybe Janine is as lonely as him. Maybe Netflix, a junk-food tabby and a shower in her kitchen are all she has. There could be common ground here that doesn't come with swings and an Alsatian. Why did he say the thing about the hives? What came over him?

After that, there's nothing Bruce can do but head into Party Palace and watch the screens tick over. He imagines a giant lasso catching hold of them and flinging them right through the plate-glass doors. He sees himself harnessing the universe and—eighth wonder of the world!—it works. At the counter he actually says, 'Just water, please.' The guy at the till, who has served him for the last four years, raises the tiny silver dumbbells in his eyebrows, so Bruce says, 'Make that two.' Make that two! Bruce *never* gets to say that.

He drinks one bottle down. The water is straight from the fridge, and it drives an icy nerve through his bone marrow, which carries him back up to Pacific Power where he flips his mat out right next to the heavy breather wearing the pants with the built-in butt lift. The heavy breather can't touch her toes, and Janine always says, 'Bring the ground up to you. If you don't have blocks, use your water bottle.' Bruce does have blocks, but the blocks won't say what he wants to say. He leans on the bottle during twisted half-moon, then at the end of class, instead of waiting to say, 'Now here's the thing,' he places the second bottle in front of her.

'For you, Janine.'

She picks it up and turns it over like it might not be what she thinks it is.

'Water,' he says.

'Yes.'

'Egg free.'

She takes a deep breath like she's waiting for the joke. Then she wanders over to the cupboard as if she's going to slam it shut again but instead, she reaches inside, takes out a ball the size of a peach and hands it to him.

'I keep getting them free,' she says. 'With online shops.'

'It's not just donuts that give you freedom,' he says. 'What do I do with it?'

'Sit on it and roll around. Try to stay upright.'

'That's it?'

'That's life,' says Janine. 'In balance, out of balance. Awkward, but persistent. Keeps you guessing.'

Next week, Bruce is back in Party Palace before class, eyeing up the Boston Cremes, because he has had so many fantasies involving the ball and Janine's deep tissues that he's pretty certain he won't be able to look her in the eye. The main window opens out onto the park, where the fabric of the cosmos is glitching. The glitch is dog-shaped and obedient. Sweetheart is letting herself be patted by a man with scalp tattoos and a hunting rifle. She has lost her rage, her thirst for blood. Bruce turns to the guy at the till and says, 'Two waters, please.'

The man with the scalp tattoo is cupping Sweetheart's face in his hands and ruffling her ears. Last time anyone ruffled Sweetheart's ears, they had to get hooked up to a bag of O positive.

'Lost your tap down the back of the sofa these days?' says the Party Palace guy, sliding the water over the counter. 'Nothing else I can do you for?'

Bruce traces J for Janine in the condensation on one of the bottles.

'No, I don't think so,' he says, licking his finger. The condensation tastes fresh as the dawn of hope.

'Sure?'

Sweetheart's tail whips this way and that, a live electric cable in a typhoon, a cosmic string that just came loose.

'Guess not,' says Bruce. 'Not unless you're the universe.'

CAROLYN McCURDIE

Intersect

At five the ferry casts off. It churns away from harbour piles,
oily murk, and out into wind-blown chop. Inside, we unbutton, doze,
as it grumbles and waddles, tips and creaks,
rolls through the winter night to a sea-slopped island wharf.

My road home winds between paddocks
and each step shifts me to a different breathing.
I turn off my torch. My skin lifts to the touch of dark-gifted
quiet, to a breeze that's sweet with pasture
and the heads-down privacies of sheep in the shelter of trees.
Inhalations of earth, dung, frost in the air.

A truck passes and with foot-slammed force, stops. Backs up.
Tumbling out comes the man who wishes me harm
and he's charging, bull-bellowing some brute incoherence
and for a micro-second it's as if I'm hung,
ectoplasm, mute, not attached to smashable flesh or bones,
no legs, no wings, no cry of alarm from grass or sheep or sky

or road—
headlights
my torch frantic in front of the wheels
car stopping
door open

and I say nothing to this man on his way home from work
except *I live there, can you drop me there,*
and *thank you, thank you, thank you.*

JORDAN HAMEL

The Monty Hall Problem

I've given you a chance, don't be scared, I've taken
one door, would you like to switch, or stick, don't worry
there are no wrong choices when you have an audience

behind one, a galaxy of denim, jeansed solar fountains,
jeansed houses, jeansed horses, jeansed junk rubbing together,
jeansed teeth chewing holes for jeansed mouths to breathe

behind another, meat worlds, with gristle goodbyes
choked down in abattoirs, over cookies, sandwiches, all the grief
food you could want, and free cups of tea sluiced through a grate

behind another, sour after-foam of unkempt beaches
all medical waste and salt debris, shell pressed to ear sounds like
compassion, quiet goodbyes shipwrecked on driftwood

behind another, three prisoners, awaiting their fates,
behind another a scorpion, another, a toad, behind another
a trolley (ignore it, that's a problem for another day)

behind another, a reality in which Dad learns to use FaceTime
before he dies, Mum will still comment on every digital interaction
(this happens behind every door, you might as well embrace it)

another, an embrace, another, not so much a door as
a clenched eyelid, another, a second trolley, it's not the same
as before, I wouldn't lead you astray, I wouldn't leave you

behind, another, a stray truth, caught mid-gasp like reflux
another, you spit it out, another, it is spat back in, another
another, a father, a mother, meat, salt, heat, junk, swallow

softness, yourself, an other, staring back with blameless
eyes and mouths like hinges, the crowd is going wild,
what will you do I know what I would do if I were you

LUCINDA BIRCH

Motherlove

Karla stands in the shower and watches as thin trickles of blood creep and kink down her inner thighs, swirl diluted pink across the white plastic and down the plug. Her stomach aches. She leans her head against the shower wall. Hot water on the back of her neck. She will not cry. She will not let herself feel anything other than relief. Later, when her partner Ben comes home she tells him she's fine. He stares at her, not quite believing, not sure if she blames him.

—It was over fast. We made the right decision. Who'd bring a kid into this mess? she says.

Ben reaches out his arms and she steps into them and they hold each other. Tight. Not quite desperate.

The evening is hot. The suburbs of Sydney broil and stink. The reek of tarmac jelly and barbecue, the air swampy and tinged with smoke. Ben sits on the back doorstep, beer can in hand; Karla wanders across the frazzled lawn to the swimming pool. Takes a big slug of wine, wades down a step knee deep into the pool, then sits on the concrete edge. She leans forward and gazes into the water. There's a shadow sliding across the deep end. Karla stands up and peers down, eyes squinting against the watery flash and glare.

—Fuck! she shouts.

—What? Ben is on his feet. He jogs over and looks into the water where Karla is pointing. The octopus in the swimming pool roams slowly around the bottom of its rectangular home. It moves like water. It moves like something melted. It ripples red like raspberry jam.

—Oh my fucking God, there's an octopus in our swimming pool.

Flocks of white corellas tumble and screech in the pale sky. A few houses down the street a man wields a chainsaw which buzzes loudly like hundreds of cicadas while in the bark-shedding gum trees hundreds of cicadas buzz like chainsaws.

The same day: In a bay south of Sydney a group of three scuba divers are attacked and killed by a pack of New Zealand fur seals while tourists watch from the coastal walkway. Fur seals are not known to be aggressive. In the South China Sea a typhoon devastates the island of Palawan. Survivors report seeing waves as high as 50 metres.

The octopus in the swimming pool is mesmerising. It swims two circuits, undulating and streamlined, then settles in a corner at the deep end, fitting itself fluidly into the angles and gradually paling. Its skin flickers shadowy light. It becomes concrete grey. It watches Karla and Ben, its large eyes round with horizontal irises, elongated rectangles of black, like empty slots you could slide into. Dark, unblinking.

—How's it surviving in the chlorine? Karla wonders out loud, and—Are they arms or legs or tentacles? What're you supposed to call them?

—Maybe we should ring the aquarium? Ben says.

—Tomorrow, if it's still there, Karla says. She doesn't know why, but she wants the octopus to stay.

The sky turns orange as the sun lowers through the curtain of smoke, ashy miasma crafted by the bush fires that edge the city. Light fades brown and hazy. Invisible crickets warble. Leaves on the big gum in the corner of the garden dangle, twist and clatter in the warm breeze. The 10.30pm flight to Singapore takes off from the airport and bellows across the sky: windows rattle, leaves drop. Karla and Ben shift two chairs to the side of the pool and sit and watch the water. The pool shines deep brown in the city light, the octopus a bruise on the bottom.

—I'm glad it's here, Karla says.

—Me too. It feels like some kind of omen, y'know, like a sign. Ben smiles at Karla.

—Is that weird?

—Nah, that's not weird. It's one of those days. Omens everywhere.

Karla rubs her stomach. Her emptied womb cramps, pain spreads like warm embers.

Overnight: A localised and unexpected storm in the Mediterranean sinks 14 fishing boats. There are no survivors. In the Gulf of Mexico, Humboldt squid in their thousands rise up from the deep ocean and swamp several squid boats. The squid attach themselves to the sides of the boats and tip them over with sheer weight of numbers. The carnivorous squid eat the drowning fishermen. The local name for Humboldt squid is diablo rojo—red devil.

It's another stinking hot day. The octopus is still in the pool, swimming languid laps. There's a wheelie bin in the pool now too, on its side in the deep end, lid open, empty. The sky glows marigold.

The man from the aquarium arrives late morning and even though Karla told him on the phone several times she wasn't joking or pulling a prank, he's surprised when he sees the octopus in the pool.

—Jesus! It's huge! The aquarium man leans forward to get a closer look.

—Amazing. Impossible, actually.

The octopus floats in the middle of the pool. It spreads its eight legs wide and reaches across the water like a tentacled umbrella, as if it understands what the aquarium man is saying and is trying to make itself look even bigger.

—Can't believe it's not dead. Fresh water, chemicals—how's this possible? He takes his phone out of his pocket, dials. You're not going to believe this, he says.

Four more aquarium people arrive in a truck. The octopus is purple. It races around the swimming pool like a metal ball in a pinball machine, it vomits dark brown ink, it thrashes and water flies from the pool in small waves. But it can't escape the nets. The octopus is bundled and hauled into a tank on the back of the truck.

—What're you going to do with it? Karla asks.

—Chuck it back in the sea. Too big for our tanks, too tough for calamari, the man from the aquarium smiles. It's going home.

—Oh, okay, Karla says. She feels bereft.

By the time Ben gets home from work the pool is clean. Karla is sitting on the edge and swinging her legs in the water. She's been swimming. The evening is no cooler than the day. The sky is still the wrong colour. The air smells of traffic exhaust and ash and toast burnt bitter. Ben gets into the pool and floats on his back, the water lukewarm.

—This is more like it, he says, hopefully.

—Yeah, I guess, Karla says.

The 6pm to Frankfurt roars as it takes off, white wings against the tangerine sky.

—Are you okay? Ben asks.

—Yeah, fine. The bleeding's stopped. I feel kind of empty though, Karla shrugs. Which is weird cos I didn't feel *full* before.

Ben feels exactly the same, but he doesn't say anything. The pool seems changed. It seems foreign and pointless now that it's uninhabited.

Overnight: A pet shop two kilometres from Karla and Ben's house is broken into. All the small animals have been taken but the fish were left untouched. Near Fiji a cruise ship is swamped by a freak skyscraper-sized wave that tosses the ocean liner as if it were a light folding of paper. Over 4500 people go down with the ship. A school of kingfish attack a small child in the shallows of a popular beach in New Zealand. Each fish is over a metre long. The child does not survive.

The octopus is back in the swimming pool. It drowses on the bottom, calm, its tentacles unfurling fronds. A guinea pig and half a white rabbit float on the surface of the water like bleeding water lilies. It's early morning, and Karla stands at the edge of the pool. The sky is beige and hazy, tepid air slides around her bare legs. Karla sips her coffee and smiles. Air New Zealand's 7.20 from Auckland flies in low and the house clatters. Cockatoos scream. A rubbish truck screeches and bangs.

Ben brings Karla a piece of toast and peanut butter. She points down into the water. Ben looks at her and grins. *It likes us*, he thinks.

Over a week: A storm in the North Sea dismantles 15 oil rigs and a wind farm. Off the Azores islands a sperm whale charges a yacht and smashes it to smithereens. A large school of barracuda surround a group of snorkellers on the Great Barrier Reef and launch a coordinated attack. A dozen swimmers are torn to shreds.

The deep end of the swimming pool is filling with trash. There are two road signs (STOP and NO PARKING), a sandwich board offering cheap haircuts, a scattering of shiny hubcaps, at least one umbrella, a bicycle, and lots of bottles. The rubbish is not just lying about; it has been arranged, interwoven and stacked. Green wine bottles twinkle and gleam.

Karla and Ben are in the kitchen making dinner when they hear a knock on the front door. Ben puts down a carrot.

—I'll get it.

There's a small child on the doorstep. A girl. She's holding out a sheet of paper. Ben glances down, sees the word MISSING printed across the top.

—Have you seen our cat? Our cat's disappeared. The little girl looks like she might cry.

—Oh, no, sorry, says Ben and he stoops to take the poster.

—And our neighbours' cat too. They can't find it either, the girl says. She sniffs.

—Oh, I'm sorry, I haven't seen any cats, Ben lies. I'll keep an eye out. Hope you find them soon. He closes the door.

Karla is standing in the hall, carving knife in one hand.

—We have to start feeding the octopus, she says.

The next five days: In Sydney Harbour eight water taxis are swamped despite setting out in calm conditions, two taken by abrupt whirlpools. The harbour swarms with sharks that devour any bodies in the water, dead or alive. Some 200 passengers on a ferry off the coast of Indonesia die when their boat is lifted by a giant waterspout, spun and tossed in pieces back into the ocean. Several pods of orca patrol Prince William Sound in Alaska, destroying every vessel they come across, including the ones moored in docks. The orca hold pieces of the wreckage in their jaws and use them to smash and batter.

Karla and Ben have taken leave from work. It's not every day you have an octopus building an edifice in your swimming pool. They set up sun umbrellas and a couple of small tables. They watch the octopus. The lawn has turned to dust, the long-dead grass seared dry and brittle. Cracks craze through it, homes for loud crickets. Magpies strut the dying lawn and jab for morsels in the crevices. Ben cooks on the barbecue, but the octopus prefers its flesh raw.

In the swimming pool the gelatinous creature carefully adjusts its architecture, its long tentacles twisting and knotting, innumerable suckers working independently in complete cooperation. An eight-brained tango of limbs. Metal is bent and shaped, bottles are stacked upright like turrets, hubcaps adorn like silver portholes. The middle of the structure is hollow. The octopus has built a beautiful cave.

Two weeks pass: A slice of the Ross Ice Shelf in Antarctica snaps off and collapses into the ocean, causing surges that destroy America's McMurdo Station and New Zealand's Scott Base. In California a series of earthquakes along the coast create multiple tsunamis, which obliterate large tracts of land and swathes of cities. Los Angeles and San Diego are partially submerged. Greenland sinks.

Karla is floating face down in the pool. The octopus has not been eating and Karla and Ben are concerned. The pork chops they throw in to the pool are ignored and float to the surface, pale and tendrilled like meaty jellyfish. The octopus doesn't come out of its cave. It lurks under the cathedral of junk, occasionally snaking a tentacle outside to curl and flex.

Karla dives and lies flat on the bottom of the pool in front of the opening. She looks in. The octopus stares straight back at her with one big eye. Its gaping siphon is opening and closing and shooting water towards the ceiling of the cave, where, dangling like bundles of glutinous white tears, Karla sees eggs. A lot of eggs. The flow of water from the siphon makes the eggs dance, and, as Karla watches, the octopus reaches up with three arms and deftly, softly, strokes them.

Karla surfaces, gasps, stands up and looks at Ben. She opens her mouth but no words emerge.

—What? Ben asks.

She takes a deep breath and tries again.

—Eggs, she says. She's laid eggs.

Karla starts to cry. She thinks she's happy. She thinks that now her life makes sense.

Six months pass: The ocean rises two metres and islands drown. Geography alters. Landslides wipe out towns and the occasional city. All airports within 100km of any coast are closed. All shipping has ceased; no boats are safe on the water. Aquatic mammals and millions of fish conduct attack after attack on any humans ignorant enough to attempt to enter sea, river or lake. Crabs snap and jab, jellies tangle and poison, sharks slice, walruses and seals crush, eels tear and strip. Even herrings bite.

Karla and Ben are now living poolside under a makeshift shelter. They are tanned and ragged and very skinny.

In the octopus's nest the eggs have changed. They are translucent, and within each glistening drop a tiny octopus is clearly visible.

The eggs have eyes.

Although they are quite hungry, Karla and Ben are content. They believe they have been chosen. They believe they are truly part of nature, rewarded by the great karmic universe for not reproducing themselves. They are the guardians of the new world. They have young to raise. Starvation may be affecting their intelligence.

The gum tree in the corner of the garden is flowering. Bright red inflorescences, star-like and fizzing. The sky is grey and full of rain, not smoke, and a gentle warm drizzle soaks the weeds and long grasses that used to be the lawn. The air smells of hot damp grass and eucalyptus and honey. There is no traffic noise. No planes split the sky. The hum of industry has been replaced by the screams of galahs, the buzz of bees, and the sound of waves. The ocean is next door.

It's the dawning of some kind of paradise.

Three months later: A series of massive earthquakes shake every continent. Mountains rupture and slide and the Grand Canyon is no longer the largest rift in North America. New Zealand is a ridge of bare mountains cutting from the ocean. Australia is a broken ring around a spreading inland sea. The planet seethes blue.

Sunshine beams on Karla and Ben. They are sitting beside the pool eating beans straight out of the cans that Ben has scavenged from empty houses further inland in the flooded city. The garden is patches of sand and overgrown shrubs, littered with heaps of seaweed from the occasional rough high tide. Butterflies of every colour flit and kaleidoscope. Seagulls caw and bicker in the big gum tree. Cicadas still shrill.

Karla stands up.

—Look! she shouts. Look! And she points into the water. It's shimmering and riffling and there's a pinky-grey stain seeping from the opening of the octopus's lair. The stain creeps and worms through the pool, the coloured water moving as if it's alive.

It *is* alive.

The pool is full of tiny octopuses.

The octopuses wriggle upwards towards Ben and Karla, who turn to each other and high-five, then hug. They are elated. The octopuses swarm out of the pool. They surround Karla and Ben like supplicants around a queen and king. Karla looks down, amazed. The tiny octopuses cover her feet, her ankles, her calves, until she's knee deep in wriggling.

One brave cephalopod climbs further, up over her knee, tickling like a fly. She leans forward to get a closer look. The little octopus sits very still and stares straight back at her, its eyes black pinpricks. More babies climb Karla's legs; one by one they ooze over and under her shorts, over and under her T-shirt. They tickle. She tries to brush them off but they stick like Velcro. They creep up her neck. Karla slaps at them urgently now, she twists and bends, picks and plucks. Ben is hopping beside her, trying to dislodge the clinging creatures from his legs and hands. One of the octopuses finds Karla's nose and inserts itself into a nostril. Too late she tries to pull it out. It's gone, sliding into her head. She shrieks once.

—Oh God! she tries to say and her mouth is immediately filled with baby octopuses. They fill her nose, her throat, her lungs. She falls, flailing at Ben on the way down. He tumbles too and they thrash around together, but not for long. Soon Karla and Ben are two motionless mounds under a gluey tide. And, soon enough, two heaps of bones and viscera. Blood dribbles into the swimming pool and rinses the lifeless carcass of the mother octopus in scarlet.

The mass of newborn octopuses moves on, a growing flood of writhing limbs and consciousness. They slither and shudder and pulse, so many heartbeats thudding as one as they pour into the ocean.

Life sinks.

Life swims.

MARY MACPHERSON

Secateurs

My father's secateurs have red-encased handles, jolly as lipstick,
curved beak-blades still sharp enough to slice whips of jasmine
snaking through trees and humidity-crazed convolvulus greedy
for every bush.

My father liked quality in his garden tools. His secateurs are stamped
Made in Switzerland.

They'd snick the stems of his heavy-lidded roses, releasing
their perfumed names as I gathered a bunch to take on the plane.
Round yellow apples from the tree stretched politely
across his balcony. He'd cook them to puffy breakfast puree.

When my brother found the townhouse on Trade Me, the second sale
since our father died, he toured every room calling out—*same, same*
then, *no—oh no—they've changed that*, as if he was keeping score
of damage to our past.

Later, I went online, and with each wrong plant and piece of furniture
the ground slipped from under me.

The northerly hisses and flies at my house. Leaves from the maple
are smashed against the shores. I nose crevices for leaf-gold
banging about with my rackety broom. I believe I can keep wood
from rot, the floor from sinking, the house from falling down.

I snip the geraniums' crisp brown heads. The blades stutter only
on marshy decay. I cut failing stems, dry stalks, diseased leaves,
torn branches. In spring I trust they'll return, like new dresses.

WAYNE YOULE

National Fuckin' Treasure

1. *Faithful*, 2023, powder-coated aluminium, 1400 x 2400mm. Private collection.
2. *Bloom*, 2023, powder-coated aluminium, 1700 x 1600mm. Private collection.
3. *Vanitas*, 2023, powder-coated aluminium, 2400 x 3600mm.
4. *House/Home*, 2023, powder-coated aluminium, 2000 x 1300mm.
5. *Act 1, Scene 7*, 2023, acrylic, oil, aerosol and enamel on linen board, 325 x 325mm. Private collection.
6. *Me and Ned | Ned and I*, 2023, acrylic, enamel and aerosol on linen board, 325 x 325mm. Private collection.
7. *Day at the Beach*, 2023, acrylic, enamel, oil and aerosol on board, 786 x 618mm.
8. *Bad luck*, 2023, acrylic, enamel and aerosol on oak veneer, 570 x 476mm.

All images courtesy of the artist and SUITE Wellington + Auckland
Photographs 1–4 by SUITE; photographs 5–8 by Dave Richards

Wayne Youle's work explores historical and current perceptions of Māori culture in order to question stereotypes and traditions. Strongly influenced by his bicultural heritage, Youle is a keen observer of the ever-shifting dynamics of Māori and Pākehā values, and his work traverses issues of identity, race, and the commodification of vernacular symbols. His practice speaks to a fascination with the visual language of popular culture, and a desire to question how history and identity are constructed. In Youle's hands, simple forms and symbols take on a historical, metaphysical and psychological weight.

The final four images presented here are depictions of Ned Kelly, the itinerant criminal and Australian national hero. Youle's depiction of Kelly as a 'National Fuckin' Treasure' is used to reflect on the idea of the character becoming bigger than the story, person-cum-mythological figure. In Youle's works, Kelly and his helmet become a caricature of Australian painter, Sidney Nolan's version, broken down to a simplified, almost comic book-style rendering. Youle's work seeks to commodify the commodified, presenting a distorted simulacrum that displaces our gaze and holds up a mirror to our consumerist selves.

—Lynley Edmeades

FRANKIE McMILLAN

This Place Could Be Beautiful

Her
That summer we ended up in the belly of a whale. Slurped down in a flood of plankton. It was obvious there'd been others living down there. 'What's with the old brocade chairs?' you said. I told you that as soon as it was high tide we could throw out all the furniture. Start anew.

You coughed every night, said the air was pungent. I sang as I cooked on the potbelly stove. Fried onion and garlic. Steamed mussels. Ba boom, ba boom, went the whale's heart. 'We could be happy here,' I said. You sat, picking at your food. You told me you'd been praying. For grass and sky, for claw and hoof, for tail and trunk. 'What are you saying, exactly?' I said. You wiped mussel juice off your chin. I threw the pan at you. Later that night you woke me. The walls had begun shaking. 'She's about to blow,' you said. You pulled me towards the baleens. I wanted to say wait, I wanted to say this place has good bones. You pulled harder.

Him
We looked around. A thick briny smell came off the old furniture. The walls dripped but it was warm, surprisingly warm. You cooked naked over the stove. You were trying to make me happy. I was trying to save us. I was trying to remember what the survival manuals said about a car filling with water. It was nothing to do with whales but it was something to do with water. I put my arms around you. Your skin was slick with grease. You turned, threw the pan at me. 'Why can't you be happy here?' you shouted. We both cried. I woke when the whale surfaced. I could feel the air pressure changing. 'She's about to blow,' I yelled. 'What are you saying, exactly?' you said. Ba boom, ba boom, went the whale's heart.

GAIL INGRAM

When I first met my grandmother,

she spoke of our shared loves, of
alpine daisies and running,
and something in her voice reminded me
of the time I spent a night in a rock shelter
with a friend I yearned for. The rain
ran down lichen-streaked walls, soaking
our sleeping bags, holding us together. Apparently,
she hadn't been as eager

when it came to her own children
and their longings, the first time
they rode their bikes with no hands,
their *look-Mum-I've-found-a-crab/a-seedpod/*
a-friend-with-benefits
she kept them at bay in the dark cave
of her moods. She never spoke of
her children to me.

By the time we met,
the black-streaked streams
of invective over a daughter's
unwanted baby had passed
and time had passed, her words
had softened—when my grandmother spoke,
I sensed she cared about me—
this young woman who appeared

so sweet.

ERIK KENNEDY

Pacific Sea Surface Temperature Anomalies

It's hotter than Venus, so everyone goes to the beach.
As sure as city traffic stops at a T,
or a $30 cocktail has too much ice,
the clammy, suffering people go to the sea.

As sure as an arsehole tells a girl to smile,
as sure as unbaptised kiddies go to Limbo,
as sure as cheap jeans stain your legs,
as sure as Russian oligarchs fall out windows,

as sure as a cooking blog is full of ads,
as sure as a sheriff fancies lethal force,
as sure as writers lie about reading Joyce,
as sure as ashwagandha tastes of horse,

as sure as carbon credits are underpriced
and dignity is expensive and love is free,
the clammy, suffering, sweltry, cynical, burned-out,
downhearted, vulnerable people go to the sea.

JESSICA LE BAS

At Puretu's Place
Arorangi, Rarotonga

You remember the snake beans,
a yard long and hanging wild in your hand,
like a ponytail severed, or fat shoelaces
Everyone in jandals. Nervous cats under
the house that fed on the junglefowl,
kittens eaten by dogs. The centipede,
as long as your foot, with its castanet clicking,
its writhing on the mat at the back door
You remember the endless heat, where
night arrived early with a crazy drunk moon
on its shoulder, a silk shawl full of stars
The deep-throated call of mangos falling
on your roof. Passionfruit, like camo-green
grenades, hiding in long grass. A competition
of crickets, all singing soprano, all looping
inside your head. Even from the back road
you heard it: the reef gulping, swallowing
down the ocean, and the roosters' crow,
that Mexican wave rolling through the night
and the next day, and one after that; all
around the round island, and the old woman
under the kuru tree sheltering from rain,
her canvas hat, her red gardening shoes,
the patience of a small island set adrift.

BRONWYN POLASCHEK

Putting the Cat Down

The moment the present slips into the past owning starts to be replaced by disowning
—Yiyun Li

We dig the grave a week before. Once we bring the body home, there'll only be a short window to get it into the ground. It'd be a mistake in this unpredictable autumnal weather to rely on a sunny day, and you never know what you'll hit when you start breaking up the soil.

The first site we plan is at the front of the house, on the path as you walk up. He often waits for us there, and we imagine ourselves thinking of him each time we arrive home. But this position is abandoned when we unearth a lurking water pipe. The second spot is up the back, between the kōwhai tree and one of the feijoas. A sunnier resting place with less foot traffic, no ablutions to disrupt, and a view. Maybe it's better for a cat in his dotage to have a bit of peace and quiet.

You can bury a cat's body in your back yard when you know you won't live in a house forever. You wouldn't scatter your father-in-law's ashes, though. It's harder to know what to do with a Marxist atheist who had no time for ceremony, than a beloved grey tabby.

These past months have meant regular visits to the vet as the cat keeps getting mysteriously thinner. His haunches started to show in January. Now it's almost Easter, and before we know the cat's prognosis, my parents decide it's time to talk about their deaths. Dad's heart is weakening, his specialist says—he'll need surgery on a valve. This is a sign to my father that detailed preparations must start. He emails my brother, sister and me a list of notable possessions and a proposed system for redistribution. On Good Friday my brother and his family drive down from Tirau, and Easter Sunday evening, still the publicly recognised day of resurrection, my original family of five sit down with cups of tea, just us, to agree on a process.

I've always unconsciously assumed any kind of planning to be inherently optimistic, a hopeful looking-forward, but of course to plan is only to anticipate a version of the future. In the one we are imagining, only some of us will be left. As we sit and talk about fairness, and sentimental connection, and practicalities, the objects at issue mutely surround us. A curated collection of belongings. A life set. I can't want any of it because of what having it will mean.

How is it best to deal with the material aftermath of a death? You can hope to be rational, reasonable and considered versions of your best selves when grief hits, but it's prudent to organise in case you are not. The truth is you might have lived your whole life eating at the same oak dinner table, or looking at a framed image of Mary and Jesus on the wall, and you might find it painful to imagine those things in your own house, but the objects collected over a lifetime will be disowned eventually, always.

As part of preparing for our cat's death, we buy two plants at Twigland—one for the earlier and then abandoned grave, which has opened up a sizeable muddy hole now slowly filling with rain, and one for what will be his actual resting spot. Two hardy perennial natives that need no attention. They are already adapted to Wellington's winds and heavy, unforgiving soil.

We adopted our cat as a sprightly one-ish-year-old who seemed unperturbed by his predicament as a new arrival at the SPCA. He was caged and quarantined from the other cats. Keen to be held though not desperate, unlike some of those we passed by. 'Hello,' his friendly eyes seemed to say. We always thought of him as a bit dim—a lover not a fighter, I used to joke—but I wonder now if he was actually just calmly wise. He knew what his priorities were.

There are ways to mark a death. You can count the years together: fifteen with our cat. Or mark time by significant events: Brexit and Trump both happened on his watch. But I measure it by the expansion and contraction of family: three children born, as well as one niece and four nephews; one parent dead, another ravaged by dementia, two left. On the day we first brought our cat home we were childless, fully parented and relatively young. Now we are none of those.

My mother-in-law, Di, was a great lover of cats—her own, and the others in her neighbourhood. She was a dedicated gardener and they were her colleagues, sleeping nearby or inconveniently digging or hunting while she tended to the prolific flowers of all varieties growing on the windy banks of her house. She'd fed our cat for us several times when we were away, driving from Hataitai and struggling to unlock our 1940s door with her arthritic hands. One of her greatest regrets was how her most beloved cat, Puss, disappeared down the bank one day and was never found. Di didn't get the chance to say goodbye or bury her or mark her grave.

Their expansive garden was long gone by the time my father-in-law, Jervis, got sick, in those few days before he died. They'd sold up years before and moved to a tidy, flat house with slippery floors, flowerless hedges and no cat. There the two had swapped roles. Once she had worried constantly over his health; now, he became her round-the-clock nurse. His body gave out in the end. A few dramatic hours after the ambulance was called, their house sat empty, interrupted only by short, rustling visits to collect up what each of them needed for their new rooms.

The things you take for a hospital stay or residential dementia care are ordinary: your warmest cardigan for cool afternoons, reading glasses and a book, slippers for cold feet, the iPad. In a hospital bed an object of value is one with utility. If you are staying longer you might bring some small items to remind you of home: photos in frames, cards, a few trinkets. But that's about all. The rest of your possessions, even those you've always treasured, will gather dust.

In his last weeks our cat's breathing becomes laboured. He begins lying in unusual spots, eyes open, watching us. The vet tells us it's terminal. She frames her diagnosis so gently you could almost miss it. As she begins quietly laying out treatment options to prolong his life, I venture the possibility of putting him down. 'Yes,' she agrees immediately and firmly, 'that would be the humane choice.' I wonder if she is trained to wait for the client to raise euthanasia as an option, or whether she has learnt from bitter experience. 'Keep him for a fortnight,' she says. 'Take some time and then book him in.'

Eventually, after my father-in-law died and Di was in long-term care, we cleared their house entirely. There was no agreed system or set of instructions. Still, the disowning was uncomplicated. Di didn't want to bother about locking the house when she was in her rambling garden so they'd accumulated little for prospective burglars to carry away, and as she felt her mind begin to unwind, she'd meticulously tidied, discarded and donated until there was even less. We were gifted her beloved Christmas decorations: the 'impossible to find' good tinsel, the antique wooden soldiers and angels, the expensive crystal ornaments bought from Kirkcaldies in town, one or two at a time over years, to create her collection.

Walking through a house of objects that are no longer owned or used is a reminder of the thingness of things. The stillness of inanimacy. A washing basket of unfolded clean sheets is no longer a task waiting to be done, but an echo of an earlier life. These objects seem smaller, less consequential, almost comic in their crumpled uselessness to the people who own them: he's dead, I want to tell the sheets; she will never change a bed again. We lock the door as we leave, the only sound our footsteps as we quietly walk away.

'Can I have your clothes after you die?' my younger daughter asks me with an appealing bluntness. She already likes to borrow my cardis. As she grows taller, the dresses will be next. I tell her she'll need to negotiate with her sister. I don't tell her that grief transforms objects. They won't necessarily be the same when I'm not here sitting on the bed as she looks through my wardrobe. I wonder if it will be easier for her to wear my Miss Crabb denim jacket if I give it to her ahead of time, with a plea to enjoy it, rather than her having to silently take it down from a hanger, alone, after I am gone.

This Easter I can happily visit my parents' home, sit on their couches, borrow their books, hug my mother wearing her clothes, but I dread encountering these objects after their deaths. The taking down and unplugging, the boxing up and sliding-off coat hangers, the emptying and folding. I imagine taking home a half-empty bottle of dishwashing liquid because it'd be wasteful not to use it, and the moment of discarding the emptied plastic into our recycling—another small gesture of thudding finality.

Time can be marked by objects accumulated, and then—if they survive the wear and tear of life—redistributed. When my father-in-law was about to be cremated, my son asked, 'Are they going to burn him in his suit?' And it's true, someone else might have wanted it, I told him, but we don't usually send people off naked. I do hope that other people are sleeping on Di and Jervis's sheets now, after we donated them. I imagine their white thick cottonness lying freshly clean in a different washing basket, full of purpose again, resurrected.

In the moment, time shifts and evades. Outside the moment it moves without relent. The arrow of time. The balm of time. All in good time. Our gradual collection of objects is just one of time's markers. The disowning of them is another.

We will dig the cat's grave. We are digging the cat's grave. We have dug the cat's grave.

He had a good life, we will remind our children to say. He was much loved. He died before he could suffer. We used the same sentiments for their grandfather, except the last.

At Easter my siblings and I agree on a plan for when my parents can no longer own their possessions. Mum listens and contributes. Dad clarifies and takes notes. We will choose in birth order, round and round, until everything important is gone. My organised sister wants a practice run, a pencilled list, but I resist. A process is abstract and light enough for me to manage. A list, even a sketched one, with its names of objects next to names of people, is not.

My mother-in-law spends the Easter holiday in her own version of time where the past, present and imagined collapse into one chaotic narrative. My father-in-law's ashes remain stored under my younger daughter's bed in their miniature pine coffin, waiting on a decision we are yet to make about where to scatter them. He'd be amused by these storage arrangements, his remains sitting next to his granddaughter's sparkly hand-me-down Doc Martens, and as someone who wasn't a great one for making decisions, I imagine he'd empathise with our indecisive plight.

Our cat lives his last days with us enjoying the autumnal sun, beautifully unaware of his fate. On Wednesday, after our 4pm appointment at the vet, we wrap his bony, delicate body, place him in the hole near the kōwhai, and cover him with earth. We bury this cat we once owned with his only possession, a striped woollen blanket. That evening we light the first fire before winter.

CINDY BOTHA

A Matter of Air

Listening for it, I'm acutely aware
of breath
how offhand we are

because now each inhale
is a skiff dragged
across ebb-tide, sinking, snagging

the hitch before her intake
is the spun-out silence
of fish in a bucket.

I want to do it for her
lie close, remind her chest to lift
make of her lungs

a pair of trembling sails
to keep her aloft.
I want to rally her body to remember

its machinery
its beautiful relationship
with air.

KATHRYN VAN BEEK

Shadow

The boy sat by the apartment window, playing with monster trucks the size of his fists.

'Bam bam!' he cried. 'You're dead!'

The mother looked up from her phone.

'What are you doing, darling?'

The boy pointed to the cat lying in a shaft of sun.

'I shot Shadow with my tank!'

The mother frowned. 'I thought they were trucks?'

The boy shook his head. 'Tanks.'

The mother came over to scratch Shadow behind the ears. Shadow's mouth opened to let out a raspy mrraow.

'Pooh!' said the boy. 'His breath smells.'

'He's old,' said the mother. 'He loves you. You love him too, don't you?'

'I do,' said the boy, putting down his trucks and nestling his soft head into Shadow's fur.

Outside, the siren went. The mother looked out the window, her gaze shooting down between rows of high-rises to the sliver of harbour at the bottom of the hill. She returned to her phone, scrolling for information.

'Look,' said the boy.

The mother looked and saw a person running through the pocket park up the hill, followed by another person, and another. A car on the street made a frantic U-turn. And there was smoke. There was smoke down by the water. As she watched, the whisper of grey grew into a growl, rising higher and thicker and blacker into the sky.

The mother used her phone camera to zoom in on the waterfront. A harsh grey shape jutted through the haze. It was some kind of ship. But not a container ship. Not a cruise ship. Not a yacht.

'What is it?' asked the boy.

'Well,' said the mother. 'I think it's a very special kind of ship. And that's why it's important that everyone knows it's arrived.' She touched the screen of her phone, frowned. 'I wonder when Daddy will get home?'

The mother moved through the apartment. Blankets were folded in neat piles on the beds. Bags were filled with clothes. In the bathroom three sponge bags, a first aid kit, a red can of petrol and a cat cage sat on the tiles. In the kitchen bottles of water and stuffed shopping bags lined up against the wall. Next to the fridge, a backpack shaped like a cat's face bulged with food and medication.

The boy drew closer to the window, trying to catch a glimpse of the special ship.

'Does it belong to them?'

'I think so, darling.'

The whirring in the mother's chest was matched by a sound. Thudding blades sliced overhead.

'Helicopter!' The boy clapped his hands. 'Our helicopter or their helicopter?'

'I'm not sure,' said the mother, but when the helicopters came into view, she saw the familiar, terrible symbol slapped to their sides. The boy saw it too, and was silent.

The grandmother waited at the library. She sat in a comfortable chair and flicked through the pages of a gardening magazine. Flick—wouldn't it be lovely to have a pergola covered in grapes! Flick—she really should get a birdfeeder to attract a circus act of tūī and kererū. Flick—and she'd love to treat herself to a hammock, so she could float through the air on warm sunny days.

At the grandmother's feet was a travel bag. The last time she'd used it, she'd been on holiday. She'd finally made it to Italy and seen the Sistine Chapel, *The Birth of Venus*, *David*, the Villa of Mysteries. The maiolica plate she'd bought as a souvenir was now carefully bubble-wrapped and stashed in the bag between layers of clothing.

'Mum!' The father stood at the entrance. He stumbled in and bent down beside her. 'What happened? I went to your house …'

But there was no house. That's what he wanted to say. I went to your house and it wasn't there. The whole street was missing. The street where I used to play. The corner shop where I used to buy lollies and lighters. It was all gone.

I went to the memorial hall where you said we'd meet if anything happened. The memorial hall was gone. I tried to call you but the call wouldn't connect. I went to the hospital. The person at reception told me to try here.

That's what the father wanted to say. He wanted to get it all straight in his head. He wanted someone to hear him and say, 'Yes, yes, that's all true, that's just how it was.'

The grandmother traced the blood, dry now, that wove down her cheek from the wound on her forehead. The father looked at the wound, and the blood, and the powdery dust on the grandmother's clothes.

'We'd better get going,' he said.

Nothing was working. Not his phone. Not the lift. The father scaled the stairs as quickly as he could, not stopping until he reached level 12. The door to the apartment was locked from the inside, so he knocked his special knock, and the mother opened it.

'The lift's broken,' said the father. 'We'll have to carry everything down.'

The mother cursed. 'I told you we should have packed the car earlier!'

In the hot silence she felt a tug on her clothes and looked down. The boy held up his little hand, splayed his small fingers.

'Matimati breathing?' he asked. He ran the finger of his right hand up his left thumb. 'Tahi …'

The mother patted the boy's head. 'That's a good idea,' she said. 'We'll do some matimati breathing in the car.'

The father bent to pick up the bags of food, then stopped. Through the windows he saw the wall of black smoke. He looked at the mother. They didn't say anything. Not in front of the boy. But the boy caught their glance.

'I can help,' he said.

'You can be the lookout,' said the mother. 'You and Shadow can keep an eye on what's happening outside.'

The mother and the father loaded themselves with as much as they could carry, then locked the boy inside the apartment and trudged down the thirteen flights of stairs to the basement carpark. It was mostly empty now. A handful of vehicles waited for their owners. Two bikes were chained to the bike rack. Food wrappers huddled at the feet of thick columns.

The grandmother waved at them from behind the windscreen. She looked small and fragile in the passenger seat—thinner and yellower than she'd been before. As the father heaved belongings into the boot, he wondered if the grandmother had shrunk in the few minutes he'd left her alone. As though whatever had hit her temple had punctured her, allowing her spirit to leak from her body like air from a life preserver.

'Everything all right?' asked the grandmother.

'Fine, thank you,' said the mother. 'We'll be back in a jiffy.'

The mother and father turned around and went back up the stairs. Five flights. Six flights. Seven. As she struggled to breathe, the mother thought of all the yoga she'd done over the years. If only she'd done spin class instead. If only she'd improved her cardio fitness. What good was core strength to her now?

At the eighth floor they paused as a young woman passed them on her way down. She carried several bags, a Pekingese dog and a large teddy bear. Her face was dewy with tears.

'Kia kaha,' said the mother, who didn't know what else to say.

'Kia kaha,' said the woman, her voice a tight string about to break.

The mother and father finally reached the twelfth floor and let themselves back into the apartment. The boy stood with his hands pressed against the window, peering out at the city below.

'Did you see anything?' the mother asked.

'Just a fire,' he said, pointing at a rubbish bin in flames in the pocket park.

The mother and father grabbed the bags and the bedding from the bedrooms, then once again locked the boy in the apartment and made their way down the stairs. When they reached the car, the grandmother was shaking.

'Shall I stay with her?' asked the mother.

'There isn't time,' said the father. They were both breathless from walking up and down the stairs. 'One last trip and we'll be done.' He handed the grandmother a bottle of water and a packet of biscuits. 'Try to eat something—it'll make you feel better.'

From within the windowless stairwell they heard a thunderous noise and felt a dreadful quaking through the building and their bodies. Though their legs were heavy and their lungs burned, they quickened their steps to get to the boy. At last they reached level 12. The mother's hands shook as she unlocked the door to the apartment. The walls were still standing. The glass was still in the windows. And the boy was still there, tracing his left hand with his right index finger.

'Toru, whā ...'

'Anything to report?' the mother asked, blinking her eyes to dislodge the mental image of the windows smashing and the boy falling, falling, falling through the sky, landing shattered on the pavement in a shower of glass.

'Yes, I saw a plane,' said the boy. His mouth twitched as though he might cry, as though he too had seen himself tumbling from the window, hurtling to the ground and snapping like plastic.

'You saw a plane? That's exciting!' said the mother. 'What did it look like?'

The boy described a pterodactyl-shaped plane with four huge propellors. The father snatched up the last of their things.

'Ready?' he asked.

'I just need to find Shadow,' said the mother. 'Come out, little miaow-miaow. Come out, pussycat.'

She found the cat trembling beneath the couch. There was no time to lure him out with treats and kind words. Instead, she and the father each lifted one side of the sofa, and the boy tackled the cowering animal. The cat's spine was an abacus beneath his fingers.

'He's so skinny.'

'I know, poor thing,' the mother said, taking Shadow and posting him into his cage, remembering the old days when he'd splayed all four legs like a god's eye against the opening, refusing to go in.

'Don't forget his insulin,' she said, and the father took the vial from the fridge and shoved it into the cat bag with an ice pack.

'Right-oh,' said the father. He handed the backpack to the boy. 'Are you ready for an adventure?'

There was a bad smell in the car.

'Shadow's done wees,' said the boy.

The mother frowned. 'I forgot the litter box. Let me run upstairs and get it.' She unbuckled her seatbelt.

'We are not taking a litter box!' said the father. 'We can barely fit our food in here! We are not taking a toilet for a cat!'

The mother bit her lip and tightened her jaw, but still tears fell from her eyes and a sob fell from her throat. The father opened the back door and took her hands in his.

'We'll be all right.'

The mother pushed past him. 'I don't think I packed all his special food.'

'That cat's more trouble than it's worth!' said the father, which was hard to argue with because it's difficult to calculate a cat's worth—particularly a cat that has to eat special food.

The father leant into the car and extracted the cage. 'Let's leave him down here with some food and water. He'll be okay.'

The mother stared at the father.

The father shrugged. 'He can catch mice. It's paradise for a cat down here.'

'Nice euphemism.'

'What's a euphemism?' asked the boy.

The mother didn't take her eyes off the father. 'It's something you might say if you want to do a bad thing,' she said.

The front door of the car opened and the grandmother got out.

'Everyone!' said the father. 'Back in the car!'

But the grandmother didn't get back in the car. She shuffled around to the father and mother, and they both noticed how hard and round her stomach was beneath her loose-fitting top.

'I've been thinking,' she said. 'I'd be more comfortable if I stayed here. I'll stay here with—'

But before her words could ring around the carpark, the father buried them. 'Absolutely not, no. We're all going. All of us. Even Shadow.'

He peered into the cat cage. Shadow stared back at him, eyes wide.

'I'd like to stay here,' said the grandmother.

The father ignored her and flicked his spare hand at the women, as though shooing chickens. 'Everyone back in the car. Let's get going.'

But the mother and the grandmother didn't move.

The father flicked his hand again. 'Come on!'

There was a loud bang and a man shot across the carpark, his shoes making a heartbeat sound on the concrete floor, the stairwell door slamming behind him. He jumped into a van and sped away.

'*Get in the car!*' the father screamed.

'I'm staying here,' the grandmother repeated. 'It's my wish.'

The father sank to the ground, his head in his hands. The mother silently rearranged the food in the back of the car, removing the choicest items—the biscuits, the chocolate, the herbal tea—and stashing them in the grandmother's bag.

'There's plenty of food still in the cupboards,' she said. 'Fill up all the pots and pans with water, just in case. And what else do you need? Medicine?'

The grandmother shook her head. 'I've got plenty of medicine.'

'Toothpaste? Soap?'

'I don't need anything else.'

The mother put on the cat-shaped backpack and hauled the grandmother's travel bag out of the car.

'Stay where you are, please,' she told the boy. 'And lie under the blanket. Hide-and-seek. Okay?'

She patted the father's bent head and picked up Shadow's cage. The father got to his feet and held his arms out to the grandmother.

'Let me carry you,' he said.

The father drove. Driving meant all he had to do was solve immediate problems: avoid blocked roads, avoid traffic jams, avoid 'them'. Driving meant he didn't have to think.

'Which way should we go?' asked the mother.

Up ahead, the sky filled with an explosion of birds. The father steered the car in the opposite direction.

The mother ran her right index finger around the contours of her left hand as she breathed. Tahi, rua, toru, whā, rima. In the back seat, the boy drove his monster trucks up and down his thighs.

'Brmm brmm brmm,' he said. And then, 'Whee-oh, whee-oh.' And then, 'When will we get there?'

'When we get there,' said the father.

There was more he wanted to say. Much more. But there were no words. No words at all.

The grandmother arranged some biscuits on her maiolica plate and set it on the arm of the sofa with a cup of tea. She sat down and took a selfie, making sure the biscuits and the teacup were in the shot, behind her smile. She sent the photo to the mother and the father. She'd heard that messages weren't getting through today, but perhaps it would transmit tomorrow.

She felt something and looked down to see Shadow scrambling onto the couch. The old cat curled up beside her, his hind legs sticking out at an arthritic angle. The grandmother smiled.

'Shadow, did I ever tell you about the time I went to Italy?' she asked.

Well, you would have loved it. That's what she wanted to say. I went to the Torre Argentina Cat Sanctuary in Rome. In the ruins of an ancient temple, old women like me looked after old cats like you. There were blind cats and two-legged cats and no-eared cats, all swimming in their own patches of sunshine. And Italy itself—well! The art, and the light, and the food, and the people ... I'd dreamt about it all my life. See the gold and turquoise colours in that maiolica plate? Those are the colours of Italy.

That's what the grandmother wanted to say, but she was too tired to say it. Instead, she closed her eyes and sank back against the cushions.

Shadow and the grandmother sat together on the couch. Outside the window, the dense black smoke rose higher. Inside the apartment, the cup of tea went slowly cold.

TESSA SINCLAIR SCOTT

Not Chickens

Not chickens, in my day we called 'em chooks, you see.
A hen is a chook. A chicken is a baby chook. And a rooster?
Well, he's just himself, isn't he, most of the time just strutting

around so proud. Anyhow, I don't like chooks, Dad says.
As a kid I'd wake to their clucking. My mother saying get up,
I will pluck and gut them you just have to kill them. Sun always

seemed to be shining vertical on my left-hand-held hatchet,
right hand holding one scrawny neck and chook screeches
ascending ragged to the blue. One chop, that's all you've got.

What I learnt was: I have one hand to hold, and one to dispatch
an Orpington black or behead a Rhode Island red and worst of all,
the white chooks, in the end my hands were deep in the same scarlet gush.

RACHEL FALEATUA

summer

rolling pink puffs of candyfloss build castles in the sky and jasmine scents rich and exotic forever alluring tempting tantalising me I bury my face deep in their blossoms drinking in their sweet scent it is so hard to drag myself away so I return again for just one more deep breath never sickly sweet always perfect the very smell of summer the scent of days where the sun has heated the concrete pavement and burns my small bare feet I run along ready to jump into the blue depths of the pool where the water folds itself around me over me through me and I lie back and look at the sky and see blue and pink wafts of joy weaving through the canvas and a lone bumblebee makes its presence known with a loud humming for the summer stretches on before me— endless and forever delightful with books to be read walks to be walked swims to enjoy and potato chip sandwiches with just a little marmite to be eaten followed by the warning words 'now don't swim for a while or you might get a stitch'

PETRA NYMAN

Lena Likes

Lena likes to dance. She rushes home from school, drops her bag on the floor and bangs the door shut behind her. She loops the lanyard with the apartment key off her neck and places it in a drawer so it doesn't get lost. Her mum has told her a million times to do that. The phone sits silent on the hallway table. Lena runs past it to the lounge. She sits cross-legged on the floor, turns on the television and inserts a tape in the VCR player. She rewinds it to the right spot and presses play. There's a click and hum as the machine begins to turn.

Lena has been waiting all day to get home to practise. At school, her teacher kept reminding her to sit still but sometimes her feet just tap on their own, or her hips sway side to side without her doing anything. Not on purpose at least. Towards the end of the day, all the teacher had to do was give Lena a look and she'd freeze. It was just that the new moves she's in the middle of learning kept looping around her mind. During the last class she concentrated her hardest on multiplication and on not moving her feet. It would have been the worst to be held back.

Lena picks at a nearly-ready-to-fall-off-scab on her knee while she studies the performance. Little speckles of brown dry skin float to the floor. Lena used to play with Tina until both their parents got home from work, but now she dances. Skyscrapers frame the stage and lights form twirling circles underneath the singers' feet. CatCat is her favourite. Even if they weren't from here they'd still be. Lena focuses on every arm circle and sidestep. The moves are easy really. She likes their nightgown-like dresses, their puffed-up hair, and the lyrics.

This year's competition was the most exciting ever, since they were allowed to sing a chorus in English for the first time. *Bye bye baby, baby goodbye.* It doesn't matter if the rest of the song is in Finnish, it still sounds better like that. This time it felt like they had a real chance to win, so it doesn't matter that they didn't. *Eurovision 1994* lights up above the stage as the song finishes and Lena presses pause.

It would be better to practise the routine with Tina, because there should really be two singers, but since she's moved away Lena has to do it on her own. Tina will probably be practising her part on her own too. Next time they see each other, maybe in the summer holidays, they can do it together. Olli from upstairs might like to learn the backup dancers' moves. Lena could go ask him. She could let him play on her Nintendo afterwards, he loves it. But he'd probably just say no anyway or laugh and tell everyone.

Lena rewinds the tape and watches the women's movements in reverse. It looks almost the same as when the tape is played normally. The phone rings but Lena doesn't like to answer it. She stops the tape and the TV screen fills with black and white spots. Lena watches the phone, holding her breath, and waits until it stops. If it rings again straight away she knows it's her mother and then she'll pick it up. The ringing stops and there's only silence and the sound of the TV static. Lena sits still for a few more minutes, then runs to the bathroom to scrub her hands with soap. Afterwards, she gets back into position in front of the TV.

She is going to get all the moves and words this time. She's going to think only about what she's doing. It doesn't matter that she doesn't have a friend to practise with. It doesn't matter if the phone rings, she just won't answer it.

Lena likes everything about Eurovision. She likes the performances, audience, the commentators and even waiting for the points at the very end. Even though CatCat didn't come first, Lena thinks they should've. Or at least second. If she practises enough, she might one day perform there herself. Her and Tina could be like CatCat and sing together. They would win for sure. Then they would give autographs to little girls like herself and have their pictures on the covers of magazines. That's what Lena dreams about.

She spends the afternoon practising the performance alone. Her sister is out and her mother works late most days. Before the calls started, she used to skip to the phone excitedly every time it rang, but now she hates it. Finally, Lena stays in step the whole way through. She smiles and claps her hands, does a few jumps up and down. Then she bends down to the VCR player and ejects the tape. She turns the TV off and hears the birds outside.

The sun is beginning to set. Lena looks out the window and can just make out the pretty little leaves budding on the branches of trees. Blackbirds sit side by side on a streetlight by the carpark and sing. Lena likes springtime.

She turns and begins to skip towards the kitchen. She'll practise once more after she's eaten, then she can show her mother when she gets home.

Lena is in the hallway when the phone rings. She stands still and stares at it. It stops and begins again before Lena has time to move, so she lifts the receiver and holds it unwillingly near her ear, but only just close enough to be sure of the voice at the other end. She doesn't want to hear the breathing again.

'Lena?' she hears her mother's voice.

'Hi,' Lena says and feels her body un-tense.

'Why can't you answer the first time I ring?'

Lena lies and says she was in the toilet.

'It's rude to pick up the phone and not say anything,' Lena's mother scolds. 'You're supposed to answer with your name. That's being polite.'

Lena knows how to answer the phone. But she doesn't want to tell him her name.

'Did you remember that I'll be home late?'

'Yes.'

'There's macaroni in the fridge.'

'I know.'

'Everything okay?'

Lena doesn't say a word. She thinks about the pad that was in her underpants the first time he called. The blood on it was not red like when she gets a cut, but dark and smelly. She can't understand why anyone would want to lick down there. She thinks it's all her fault.

'Lena?' she hears her mother call.

'Mum.'

'Yes?'

There's a pause.

'Can I have some dessert?'

'Have a piece of fruit, not anything sweet. It's healthier.'

Lena hears a murmur of someone talking to her mum through the line.

'Honey, I need to go. See you later tonight, okay?'

'Bye, Mum.'

Lena lowers the receiver and hears her mother say something just as she sets it down with a click. She lifts the receiver back, but there's only the hum of the dial tone.

Lena goes to the bathroom, scrubs her hands again and heads back towards the kitchen. She pulls out an oven dish from the refrigerator and sets it on the bench. Plump drops of water have formed underneath the plastic wrap and Lena likes to run her finger along it, letting the drops drip down one by one. She dishes herself a plateful of macaroni, all the while shifting her legs in sidestep and mouthing the words to the song. She puts the plate in the microwave, pulls the wrap back over the dish and places it in the refrigerator. The phone rings again and Lena side steps back to it. She thinks it's her mother and lifts the receiver right up to her ear.

DAVID EGGLETON

After Reading Eleanor Catton's *Birnam Wood*

Lady Macbeth's roses are bloody
warriors, raised in a vase;
her wine has body,
and is heart-warming red, through and through.
The king in his cardboard burger crown
is feeding half the town dump
with a leftover seagull cull;
his bloodied hands point
this way to the recycling depot,
that way to the trash compactor;
and the bright carbuncles
on the backsides of tin hides of cars
are winking their turns left and right
into the McMansion maze
of Birnam Wood, where each suburban subaltern
in real-estate uniform
readies the trampolines of screens,
as a sudden sob-sister's siren call
ferries another fallen queen
to the ambulance bay of a hospital.

CATHERINE TRUNDLE

Four Haiku for My Son

a pink uterus
unused, sits on the top shelf
in a Christmas tin

hand me the baby
sew your grief into the red
lining of my shoes

a scaffold stronger
than the monument within
climbs like a spider

unguided missile
weapon of mutually
assured construction

Dawn Net

We work against
the suck of tide
drag up a body

of water, the fish shoaled in
Rest it against the bank
Our method of bounty is clean

Toss baby sharks, fish fluted
with bright lice
Fingers hug the gill line

Be mercy. Be a sickle
and they won't feel it blading in
to tear a vision of you

Work your intentions inside
Segregate fillet from bowel

Gentle. Nicked guts smell
sour, like birth, or skip juice

Now rinse in seawater
Wash the killing out

MACKENZIE SMITH

untitled

lifted from Taupō's moors, the fragment of ice is already an image receding. let the memory slip and it will shatter like glass. know that it did not begin here, with the cold sun seeping through my outstretched hands, but with the desire to archive this moment. for to say, by way of a missive, that x was an archive was to possess all that x contained; and as archivists, we were as demarcated as what we presided over, the very image of the planet. but that's the problem with circumscription, right? you draw a circle, everything follows the centre, the poet forgets this is an exercise in seeing, not in claiming; that the poem is struck through with an erasural current, that x indexes its destruction. like a star that fell out of step with its pulsation, this was a memory for forgetting. I cup my face to the window, inside it's raining. there's a mirror in the hallway: her form, obsidian.

geoglyphs

below the prison colony, a sliver
cuts through the well like starlight
the coin is a splinter in the fabric of the pool
as lucidity is for the dreamer
they had carved their names into rock
a hieroglyphic trail at the edge of the world
as if to ask, what wounds can be written
without time?
/
today our hands are slow, burdened
by winter's quiet passage
by our shared predicament
our host, K, says we don't need to fear the fox
and its nightly visits, luminous & ethereal
we need things, he says, we don't yet know we need
later, I find this message inscribed into the toilet floor
glistening

REIHANA ROBINSON

You Knew

You knew everything about fucking and kava—
a girl in every port like a roving sea captain

I'm making some of this up
It starts out brutal as the child of spies

I'm caught between anger and a voice like prayer
But truth is fragile and memory tricky

Fragile like a boy's heart sticky with sea salt
A surfer with true friends in world corners

like Mo'orea, Tananarive, Cap d'Antibes
Nouméa, Port Vila, Paris, Manoa …

Traces, flecks of memory lie in Mokulē'ia and
Paia, Kaimuki and mists of Haleakelā

You are an unidentified seamount chain
rising like a small god into the play arena

East meets West and it's all underwater
and masculine and glowing like the young

volcano you are. To lose this rudder—
I would craft myself un-*triste*

but *vraiment désolée* I cannot
It can be good. It can be bad

Annie was right all along
Tu vas me manquer

CADENCE CHUNG

The Immaculate (after Schumann)

I've always thought that's the problem with poets—they want everything to be transcendental, want a snog to be more than a snog. Everyone always craves the purest motivations until all you get are love letters and wet kisses and suddenly you realise you were after wanton all along. I touch your body like I touch my own—with a foolish sense of grief. I'm one of those idiots who makes a beeline in antique stores for the cardboard boxes of letters and postcards, pulling them out one by one, weeping. *Who were they?* I cry. *And where did they think all these words would go?* Now that I think about it, though, novelists really have the same problem, thinking that a story is something you can just put on a page. Is there really anything else to do but forgive each other? In all those requiems I used to sing, everyone is forgiven. Everyone is transformed.

The Rose-bearer

I can't be a real purist, because every time
we went to see the symphony orchestra all
I cared about was her. I've never listened to
Strauss and I frankly don't give a damn about
Beethoven and his battle of light against dark.
He can go do that somewhere else. I'm tired
of art. I'm tired of seeing a kiss in stanzas,
every touch an iamb on the skin. You know,
I keep thinking about all those old poets.
All those letters they wrote to each other. Did
they really mean them? I wonder if writing about
love changes it. I wonder if the best love isn't
written down. I wrote dozens of love letters
but god knows that I wasn't in love, not truly.
I think about telling this to the man handing
out plastic samples of wine at the supermarket,
but he looks busy and I shy away. Anything free
in life always seems too good to be true. And
do you know how much money I wasted, going
to the orchestra every weekend?

MARISA CAPPETTA

Casanova's Shirt

Casanova's shirt is woven
from bioluminescent sea creatures.

At night it is a bodiless fabric torso.
Crowds part when it strides the boardwalk.

By day it pumps iron at the muscle beach
and does handstands in the sand.

Flexes invisible biceps. Veins bulge,
strain the sleeves. The cuffs

playfully fondle bikinied women.
Wives forgive when it runs for office.

These offences are excused by the mitigating
circumstance of a well-pressed collar.

At sunset Casanova's shirt
is a silhouette in scorpion pose.

However, it begins to wrinkle, the material frays
to the dismay of the last of his living cohort.

They implore the sail maker to mend
their idol, but to no avail.

Cloth unravels when the phosphorescent
portunids release their grip.

Eyes visible and watchful, they
burrow backwards into the coastline.

CHRISTOPHER YEE

Intruders

The house perched on the crest of a steep road. From the deck you could see hills in the distance and other houses smeared across them like butter on toast. The smallest bedroom had snow-capped mountains painted on the walls, gold and silver pins pressed into the door. Kyle said he liked the carpet, its soft dark fibre. 'Imagine,' he said. 'Carpet.' Their apartment had wooden floorboards and concrete walls. It was on the third floor of a building that once housed lawyers and insurance brokers. They lived easy there, but then Kyle turned forty and became dissatisfied. He wanted to carve out a life that would sustain their future. No more blowing cash on fancy dinners and month-long holidays. They had to buy a house. It was a decision that Jordan went along with. He didn't wonder whether it was a good move for them because it seemed like the natural thing to do, the next logical step in their relationship.

The house they settled on was twenty minutes by train from the central city, the furthest out they've ever lived. Their housewarming was an intimate dinner party with friends. Jordan braised beef cheeks in red wine and served them with clumps of buttery mash. Afterwards, they stood outside with their drinks and watched the sky turn orange, then red, then black. 'Summer smells different out here,' Kyle said in a wistful tone, and their friends snickered quietly. He was always saying weird shit, but Jordan knew he was right. Summer out here smelt of cut grass, barbecue smoke, sweat under your arms. It smelt of languid evenings wandering suburban streets as a child until it was too dark and too late to stay out. When everyone left, when it was just the two of them, Jordan exhaled whatever he'd been holding in his gut since they emptied their bank accounts. Yes, he thought, we made the right decision.

Then winter hit. The biting cold, the rain, seemed to transform the house from the inside. A dank, pungent odour sprang like water from a burst pipe, dousing the walls and carpet in its stench. Jordan recognised the smell, that old foe, from his student days living in damp, uninsulated flats. He borrowed an old dehumidifier from a friend and set it up in the hallway. After the first night it was almost filled to the brim with stale-smelling water. He told Kyle he felt like they had been tricked.

'How so?' Kyle asked. But Jordan didn't elaborate.

Other aberrations appeared. Black spots on the bathroom ceiling arranged in an ever-growing spiral. Sodden patches on the carpet. Rotted wood under the deck. But worst of all were the mice that took up residence in their roof. Jordan first heard them in the middle of the night, their tiny claws scratching the sheetrock. Kyle climbed into the roof to investigate, but all he found were panels of fibreglass and a thatch of wooden beams.

There was disagreement about how to handle the intruders. Jordan wanted them eradicated, but Kyle said, 'Maybe just let them run around up there if they're not coming into the house proper.' When Kyle was a student, he'd been part of an animal rights group that spent their weekends parading angrily through supermarkets while their leader held a speaker blasting the anguished cries of factory-farmed pigs. Though he'd long extinguished his radical flame, Kyle's deep compassion for the plight of animals often caused him to take hard stances. Last year, for his fortieth, they wasted so many weeks arguing about the catering (Kyle insisted on a vegan menu) that other more important things (like finding a venue) weren't finalised until days before the event. Jordan didn't want to go through something like that again and decided it was easier to let Kyle have his way.

As if sensing their leniency, the mice grew bolder. Jordan and Kyle didn't just hear scuttering, but also scratching, squeaking, and the sound of small, hard objects being dropped or rolled across the ceiling. Jordan had to put on headphones and a true crime podcast when he went to bed. One night he dreamt that hundreds of mice had invaded the kitchen. The floor became a writhing mass of grey and black fur. He pulled a knife from the wooden block and, with extreme prejudice, started stabbing. When he woke, he could still hear the *squelch, squelch, squelch* of the blade striking furred flesh and the podcast host's measured voice describing a murder scene.

'I don't think I can take it anymore,' Jordan said. 'We have to get rid of them.'

'They're not hurting anyone.'
'Me!' Jordan said. 'They're hurting me.'

They were having dinner when the lights started flickering. Neither of them said anything, hoping it was a momentary event. But then the lights flared and everything went dark for a couple of seconds before the pale glow resumed and stabilised. Both scoured the internet for possible explanations. There were many. Faulty bulbs. Something to do with the power grid. A random power surge. Loose wiring.

'Uh oh,' Kyle said, and forwarded a blog to Jordan's phone about the dangers of rodent infestation. The blog said that sometimes mice got into the walls and messed with the wires, causing lights to flicker. Jordan did more research and found a news article with the headline 'Mouse burns down house'. There was a photo of the titular house blackened and gutted by fire. The second storey had collapsed and a stream of brick spilled onto the granite driveway. Inside, walls peeled and shrivelled like charred skin. Jordan scanned the article. A mouse had chewed on the wiring and started an electrical fire. The house was in flames within seconds. Jordan said, 'No way I'm risking this. We're getting rid of them.'

'But winter is nearly over. Then they'll be gone.'

'We're not going to debate this. The decision has been made.'

Jordan bought plastic traps from the hardware store. Prised open, they looked like the hungry mouths of alligators. He smeared them with peanut butter and set them in the roof. 'The guy said they are quick and humane,' Jordan assured Kyle, but Kyle remained unconvinced.

They caught a mouse on the first night. Jordan retrieved the trap and released the limp, grey corpse into the outside bin. 'So small,' Kyle said. 'They're so small and cute.' After the second night, Jordan found two more dead mice waiting for him. A third trap had gone off but had no body in its vice grip. Instead, there were splatters of blood and a single foot, red and chewed, beside the plastic trap. Jordan deduced that the trap must've snagged the creature's leg, forcing it to commit self-mutilation to free itself. It was probably close by, huddled somewhere dark and out of reach, dead or dying. He decided not to tell Kyle.

They continued to catch more mice throughout the week, and as the body count mounted, the scurrying and scratching in the roof naturally diminished. Gone too was Jordan's initial squeamishness. Retrieving and disposing of corpses was as natural to him as cutting into a chicken or peeling a slimy slice of bacon from the packet for frying. The mice were like the spots of mould on the bathroom ceiling that he had to spray with bleach and wipe away every weekend.

Kyle never said anything, but disapproval was smeared on his face whenever Jordan climbed down from the roof with a dead mouse. He kept his distance and his arms folded. Sometimes he would sigh softly or shudder when Jordan unclasped the trap and let the mouse fall and land with a soft thud in the rubbish. Jordan suspected Kyle didn't protest because he was also benefitting from the killing, like a mob wife who looked the other way to maintain a certain lifestyle. It made Jordan feel a little resentful and petulant, being saddled with the dirty work.

Kyle called him in the early evening. Jordan was in Christchurch for a conference and had locked himself in his hotel room to finish a report that was due in the morning. But he kept getting distracted by videos of cats attacking their owners or drag queens lip synching. His notes, handwritten on screeds of torn notepaper, were sprawled across the bed in an order discernible only to him. The day had been long, his right hand was sore from scribbling for hours with a spindly pen, and he was tired and irritated and stressed and ready for sleep.

'Hey,' Jordan said. 'What's up?'

'I just got home and there's a mouse in the bucket.'

'What bucket?'

'The one in the laundry. I came home and heard this weird noise and I went to go see what it was and there's a fucking mouse in the bucket. I don't know how it got in there, but it's trapped now and it's trying to scramble up the sides but it's too slippery and what do I do, what do I do with it? Do I let it go?'

'No, don't do that. It'll just come back into the house. You know what you have to do.'

There was a long silence.

'Kyle?'

'But it's so small and helpless.'

'Well, you can just leave it in there until I get back.'

'No, that's cruel. Okay, I can do it. But what do I do? What's the most compassionate way to do this, do you think?'

'I don't know about compassionate, but the easiest is probably to drown it.'

'Jesus Christ.'

'Just pour some water in there, walk away, come back half an hour later and presto.'

'Will you stay on the phone while I do this?'

'Sure.'

Jordan listened to Kyle turn on the tap, fill something with water and carry it to where the mouse presumably was. He could hear Kyle's short, rapid breathing and wondered where on his body he kept the phone. Jordan stood by the window and looked out at the pitch-black Christchurch night. Tomorrow was forecast to be clear and frosty, so he made a mental note to not rush out of the hotel in the morning and risk slipping on black ice.

'Okay, I did it,' Kyle said. 'I filled the bucket about a quarter of the way up.'

'What's the mouse doing?'

'Paddling in the water.'

'It'll tire out soon enough,' Jordan said. 'Just go watch an episode of something and come back.'

'I feel like a monster.'

'You're not. You're doing the right thing.'

'It's so small and helpless and I'm a giant piece of …'

'For fuck's sake, just man up all right? Man up!'

There was a long silence before Jordan said, 'Sorry.'

'I'll see you tomorrow night,' Kyle said brusquely and hung up.

Whenever Jordan was away from the house for a time, whether for a few days or a few hours, the dank, damp, mouldy smell would punch him in the face with rejuvenated force when he returned.

'Hello,' he called out and leaned his suitcase against the wall. 'Kyle?' Jordan checked the bedroom, the bathroom, but the house was empty. Normally, he'd let Jordan know if he was going out, but Kyle had been silent since their phone call last night. He didn't even acknowledge Jordan's text letting him know the plane had landed safely in Wellington.

Jordan went into the laundry and saw the bucket. He switched on the light and peered in. There was still water in there, and a lifeless mouse drifting across the surface. The light glinted off the rodent's glassy eye, which was dark as obsidian. Jordan knelt for a closer look and the eye, despite having no life behind it, seemed to catch his and their gazes locked like lovers. Everything around him fell away until all that remained in the universe was him and the mouse and its pitch-black eye.

The mouse twitched. Jordan yelled and fell back and landed on his arse. His foot shot forward and knocked the bucket to its side. The water spilled onto the laundry floor, carrying the mouse to between Jordan's legs. He looked at it. It was dead. It was definitely dead. It was long dead. What he had seen before, what he *thought* he had seen before, was only his imagination.

And yet he couldn't take his eyes off it, fearing that the moment he averted his gaze the mouse would leap to its feet, shake off the water and dash for the door.

SOPHIA WILSON

a (s)mothering a dunking a beating

I can barely articulate that profound anaemia
losing blood, the full crimson orb
of it

      loosing mind from its womb
      holy infant
      my crumbling precipice

words birthed in wilderness
wild postnatal nocturnes with their overtones
of gorse and gorging

spilling tongues split the milky night
sweating and quaking, an insistent wailing

I am torn at the tenderest seams
this is isolation in the extreme—
devoid of quiet solitude

in the attrition of rest—the rest: career / self
—usurped. I am burdensome belly
beast of burden, biological breast
and you, are utterly beloved, Baby

      ★

we write to save ourselves—
desperate sewing-ups of history

> botched repairs
> plastic-coated scar tissue
> glossed-over trauma

pressured thoughts, I find a water pipe
crawl its salty lumen to the chamber
where I shed a father's missionary position—
> spew across the pane

I am ashamed of how my wits end
in elevations and depressions
the inflamed fissures of hope and fear
derailments at the bends

⋆

> time passes
we partly mend

one morning
the babies fly away

leaving in their wake an empty nest—
emptiness
a vast, quiet ache

THERESE LLOYD

Fumer Tue!

Mum calls to tell me about a nightmare—
Her and Dad preparing finger-food for a party
at our old house in Napier
the food completely covered in ants.

I'm thinking about this
as I climb Wellington's endless Dixon Street steps
past the place where a man once translated for me
into French the health warning on a packet of Rothmans.
He read it aloud, softly.
It took longer than it should have
but I was drunk and needed somewhere to stay the night.

Napier summers were unbearable. Shimmering landscapes
of inescapable pressure, heat in waves
and one unswimmable ocean.

My siblings and I under doorways in the middle of the night
riding out tremors and making survival jokes.
The earthquakes eventually shaking themselves away
leaving fluttery memories in our bodies.

The ants. Battalions of them in every corner
invading biscuit tins and bread bins. The time Mum
accidentally ate a square of chocolate covered in them.

That biting into a chocolate and finding movement
and an unexpected texture in your mouth
would carve a pathway in your brain makes sense.
Shock, like loneliness, leaves indelible tracks.

That all these years later, past Napier
past parties, past Dad,
the ants return, leaving uric acid trails in my mother's dreams.

Lifetimes within lifetimes within …
Once, my sole criteria
for the perfect man was a beard and a dog.
Now I'd settle for just a beard. Or goatee.

Entire decades spent holding in my gut, wearing lipstick.
I saw him the other day, the Dixon Street translator,
25 years later. We quietly chose not to recognise each other.

There is nothing to fear in this tiny town.
I am neither bigger nor smaller than it—
I inhabit it like a tree inhabits a park.

And all its memories, like the clouds,
are snagged in the high branches.

JESSICA ARCUS

Sex and Hummus

I have had hair reminiscent of Medusa's
but instead of snake heads, dexterous
hands could be seen reaching from the tips.
I engineered a way of holding
the heaviest of weights—knitting together
the innermost hands, felting the fingers.

Here I would hold dense things like his
stuck-in-a-meaningless-job doom-clouds or
the menacing questions—am I fucking
up my children's futures? and is our life/
boat weighted too much to one end and
if so, what needs to be thrown Kraken-ward?

I would leave the outside ring of hands
unbound, free to carry lesser weights like dates
of dance recitals, when we last had sex, so when
we should next have sex, last week's uneaten home-
made roast pumpkin hummus, the knowledge of
which socks are tolerable today etc.

A groaning in the ship's hull warned that it was
unwise to carry around that much weight and so,
slowly, slowly, I learned to draw my cutlass, while
little hands rose in disbelief, opened in surrender
—around me, a clattering, and the crackle of doom-clouds
distancing, the smell of the ocean and
                                    sex and hummus.

ZOË MEAGER

Spring Pudding

As soon as breakfast is swept from the table, Mother hangs an apron around my neck. I stand on a stool and she recites, 'Three cupfuls of ducklings.' I scoop them into a big baking bowl. Why not ducks? I wonder, but don't ask—she's busy beating crickets from the thistles.

The crickets are the mottled colour of raisins and cream, and they like to jump. My baby brother in his highchair claps each time they land: on the flour sack and the windowsill, the butter churn, the rafter, and the kettle.

'Three cupfuls of flour,' Mother says brightly, and I sprinkle it in from a height. The ducklings scoot about the bowl, cheep-cheeping and dust-bathing in the flour. I watch their yellow down turn mellow, follow strange rake-marks left by their paddle feet.

'Right? Then a thistle per head.' Mother plonks them down beside me and I nestle the thistles in.

I watch the nubby wings of the ducklings twitch as they settle to sleep in the flour. I scroll soft knobs of butter and plop them in, scoop loving dollops of jam. Mother lifts the dish gently into the oven. A pretty pudding: the snowdrop white, the blossom pink of spring.

MEDB CHARLETON

Anecdote of the Erotic

A tūī sings to god on a branch
in seven languages,
a god that will let her have her way,
lessen this need that feels like a pain
that was once there.
She shakes, pulsing with effort,
her sublime pride
in night-green feathers
and white cravat swallowed
to launch multilingual pleas
into the void of vines and trees,
over canopies discharging florets
like candy or, for some, confetti,
though *The Marriage of Figaro*
is not part of her collective mind.
She undertakes a job she never signed for,
visits kānuka in creams,
pink pūriri strands
and the fluffed red rātā
(forgiving its strangulation
of a dying host),
because nectar is treacly and gold
and best of all for free.
But she will always choose
survival over desire
when, stalking some insecure,
unnameable thing,
a man walks into a clearing
like he's walking into a house
he built with his own time,
with some companion in mind
and makes out a whistle
and the short shrift of wings.

RHIAN GALLAGHER

Caselberg Trust International Poetry Prize 2023 Judge's Report

Judging the Caselberg Trust International Poetry Competition has been a polyphonic experience: there was such a multiplicity of voices and variety of approaches to how a poem might be made. The diversity and the level of accomplishment made it a real pleasure to read and engage with the entries. Competitions are often a prompt for getting a poem completed and I'm grateful to everyone who did just that, and then submitted their work.

The role of judge might well conjure damnation and court rooms. Yet poetry competitions in various forms, in different cultures, have gone on for centuries. There have been eras in which poets literally sang for their supper. These days, no matter how well a poet sings it will rarely pay for their supper. Yet we go on singing.

Judging the competition was also hard. After several readings I had a long shortlist. I then attempted to come up on these poems by surprise, reading each at random moments throughout a day, as if there were no competition but simply my experience as a reader. Thank you again to all those who entered.

Joint Winner
'Aloneness' by **Tim Saunders** is a quiet, spellbinding poem. It's a small poem with a big interior and, in that, exemplifies something only poetry can do. It's a poem of great economy. A child listens to the distant thunder 'resound like a lonely kākāpō', the grandfather describes lekking (a breeding display performed by some male birds and mammals). The interlocking of images is done with grace: the grandfather (lekking himself?) booms for his lost wife, echoing the lonely kākāpō. The child's own sense of aloneness is melded throughout. There is no over-description, every word counts and the details are exacting: 'eroded gullies / moist and windborne'. It felt to me that the poem arrived naturally at the insight in the stunning last stanza. Far from

summarising, it led to an air of reflection: sitting with the poem, in that way you do, when you know you've been given a gift.

Joint Winner
'The Tiriti Translator' by **Jilly O'Brien** conjures a historical period with deftness and cinematic clarity: 'I knew it was Sunday / for the kirk-going carts / wore Sunday shirt with collar and tie'. This is a poem that has found its form: a lilting rhythm, apt use of rhyme and Scottish dialect so wonderfully employed: 'hand-habble' (business done quickly with a haughty air), 'buttery-lippit' (smooth-tongued). The meaning of these phrases can be intuited from the soundscape of the poem (though I did eventually look them up). The ironic slant on missionary zeal is all the more poignant because it is almost quietly given: 'You weren't to know we brought Sunday to you'. Pākehā parcelled up the land and equally chopped time into hours and days of the week. The undercut in the last stanza is beautiful: 'the river puts her fingers in her ears'.

Runner Up
'The Time of the Wetlands' by **Megan Kitching** is a lucid invocation of a wetland, built of specifics rather than generalities. The detail is wonderfully observed and shows a real feeling for place: 'a felted plain / with its tents of tussock'. The intertwining of sound and image enacts the interconnection of life forms in the habit itself: 'clouds / breathe into wind- / bruised water'; 'riroriro … slinging his concentric songs / like skimmed stones over the marsh'. The poem is attentive to life forms in the wetland and it asks us, as readers, to attend. Imbued with a meditative rhythm, so fitting for this micro-world where 'Time layers down'.

Highly Commended
'Still life in an op shop' by **Nicola Easthorpe**. How rare it is to find humour in a poem that is also seriously concerned with the climate crisis. The deadpan humour here is delicious. There is no overstatement; the poem sticks within the constraints it has established and unfolds like a scene in a play. Beguiling, acerbic and funny. It touches on intergenerational dissonance and I doubt whether I will ever get the image of 'glitter tipped fingernails shaped like long coffins' out of my head.

TIM SAUNDERS

Aloneness

Sometimes I would stay
with my grandfather
and listen
to thunder's distant rumble
resound like a lonely kākāpō
down valleys
and eroded gullies,
moist and windborne
through the green velvet crush
of undergrowth.

Under a half-pie moon
he described the meaning of lekking
and talked of
nocturnal behaviours,
the uselessness of wings,
the scattered moss
that crept across headstones
and the south side of rātā.

On the shelf
above the fire
were my grandmother's ashes.

Some nights
my grandfather scooped a bowl in the dust
and boomed for her.

JILLY O'BRIEN

The Tiriti Translator

The swings were all chained
and the sea salt was finer
so I knew it was Sunday

I knew it was Sunday
for kirk-going carts
wore Sunday shirt with collar and tie

I watched their fury flash by
but the sea was our kirk
and a bou-backit sea requires work

even on a Sunday.

You weren't to know we brought Sunday to you
when we came, hand-habble, to shoot kererū
travel upriver, harvest the moon

and the stars, buy land at the market
buttery-lippit, for a penny an acre
singing by afternoon

the tune of the righteous, the pious
the greedy, the liars, firm
in the truth of the written word.

Still, harken Tūī the parson bird
making the sound chains make
when they shake to the ground

Chain sounds part of his repertoire
the heart of resistance
Ko te Rātapu tēnei rā

The river puts her fingers in her ears
rolls the stones over and over
and over and over

even on a Sunday

MEGAN KITCHING

The Time of the Wetlands

Scry into a sinkhole: a felted plain
with its tents of tussock
in the wake of night

porous with sky

gleams, hums. Here clouds
breathe into wind-
bruised water and rare moments

come clear, as the chord
of a duck drawn across a pond.

In secret pockets

moves the juggler's shadow of a hare
or riroriro on a flax stalk
slinging his concentric songs

like skimmed stones over the marsh,
the groans of geese,
cymbals of light.

Silence blows south-west.

The thousand lashes of toetoe,
harakeke blink
repeatedly blink.

Time layers down.
Matted shallows swallow
the whirlpool of the sun.

The Landfall Review

Landfall Review Online

www.landfallreview.com

Reviews posted since April 2023
(reviewer's name in brackets)

April 2023

Comrade: Bill Andersen: A communist working-class life by Cybele Locke (Philip Temple)
The Last Letter of Godfrey Cheathem by Luke Elworthy (David Herkt)
A Runner's Guide to Rakiura: A novel by Jessica Howland Kany (Elizabeth Heritage)
The Wandering Nature of Us Girls by Frankie McMillan (Kay McKenzie Cooke)
Songs to the Unsung by Kayleen M. Hazlehurst (Piet Nieuwland)
The Wanderer: Book two by Ron Riddell (Piet Nieuwland)
Albatross Neck: Landings by the ancient mariner and romanticism in Aotearoa New Zealand 1770–2022 by Nigel Brown and Denys Trussell (Piet Nieuwland)

May 2023

Ruin and Other Stories by Emma Hislop (Airini Beautrais)
Kāwai: For such a time as this by Monty Soutar (Michael O'Leary)
Alice in Therapy Land by Alice Tawhai (Gina Cole)
Dirge Bucolic by Jasmine Gallagher (Erik Kennedy)
Always Italicise: How to write while colonised by Alice Te Punga Somerville (Erik Kennedy)
We Enter The by Piet Nieuwland (Erik Kennedy)
Under a Big Sky: Facing the elements on a New Zealand farm by Tim Saunders (Lawrence Patchett)
Towards a Grammar of Race in Aotearoa New Zealand eds Arcia Tecun, Lana Lopesi and Anisha Sankar (David Eggleton)

June 2023

The English Text of the Treaty of Waitangi by Ned Fletcher (Paerau Warbrick)
A Month at the Back of My Brain: A third memoir by Kevin Ireland (Alan Roddick)
So Far, For Now by Fiona Kidman (Nod Ghosh)
Tales from the Wood's Edge: A memoir by Wilma Laryn (Nod Ghosh)
Paper Cage by Tom Baragwanath (Tina Shaw)
O me voy o te vas / One of us must go by Rogelio Guedea with English translations by Roger Hickin (Lindsay Rabbitt)
Rāwaho/The Completed Poems by David Howard (Lindsay Rabbitt)
Prayers for the Living & the Dead by Lindsay Rabbitt (Siobhan Harvey)
Still Life: Timeless poems by Helen Jacobs (Siobhan Harvey)
Stream Light by William Direen (Siobhan Harvey)

July 2023

Crazy Love: A novel by Rosetta Allan (Elizabeth Heritage)
The Deck by Fiona Farrell (Owen Marshall)
Eddy, Eddy by Kate de Goldi (James Norcliffe)
No Rising of the Sheep by Bill Bradford (Harry Ricketts)
Selected Poems by Andrew Johnston (Harry Ricketts)
The Tip Shop by James Brown (Harry Ricketts)
A History of New Zealand in 100 Objects by Jock Phillips (Nicholas Reid)
Though Shaded Glass: Women and photography in Aotearoa New Zealand 1860–1960 by Lissa Mitchell (Mary Macpherson)

August 2023

Histories of Hate: The radical right in Aotearoa New Zealand eds Matthew Cunningham, Marinus La Rooij and Paul Spoonley (Victor Billot)
Ithaca by Alie Benge (Andrew Paul Wood)
Home Is An Island: A writer's tribute to the islands of Aotearoa New Zealand by Neville Peat (Tim Saunders)
BITER by Claudia Jardine (Liz Breslin)
The Pressure of All That Light by Holly Painter (Liz Breslin)
HEAL! by Simone Kaho (Liz Breslin)
The Spanish Garden by Cliff Taylor (Michael O'Leary)
Back Home in Derry by David McGill (Michael O'Leary)
Tauhou by Kōtuku Titihuia Nuttall (Robyn Maree Pickens)

September 2023

Katherine Mansfield's Europe: Station to station by Redmer Yska (David Eggleton)
Downfall: The destruction of Charles Mackay by Paul Diamond (David Herkt)
A Kind of Shelter Whakaruru-taha: An anthology of new writing for a changed world eds Witi Ihimaera and Michelle Elvy (Rachel Smith)
Past Lives by Leah Dodd (Genevieve Scanlan)
Sea Skins by Sophia Wilson (Genevieve Scanlan)
This is a story about your mother by Louise Wallace (Genevieve Scanlan)
Deep Colour by Diana Bridge (Genevieve Scanlan)
The Artist by Ruby Solly (Loveday Why)
Foxstruck and Other Collisions by Shari Kocher (Loveday Why)
Iris and Me by Philippa Werry (Loveday Why)
The Fate of the Land Ko ngā Ākinga a ngā Rangatira: Māori political struggle in the Liberal era 1891–1912 by Danny Keenan (Tom Brooking)

Other Forms of Dreaming
Emma Gattey

Te Kaihau | The Windeater by Keri Hulme (Te Herenga Waka University Press, 2022), 272pp, $30; **Dick Seddon's Great Dive and Other Stories** by Ian Wedde (Te Herenga Waka University Press, 2022), 256pp, $30

Originally published in 1986, the year after *The Bone People* won the Booker Prize, *Te Kaihau | The Windeater* is a delirious, taut, musical collection of Keri Hulme's shorter work. It spans 20 stories in which the characters and their life-sway speak to her own whakapapa: Kāi Tahu, Kāti Mamoe, Orkney, English. In 1985 Hulme wrote:

> Telling stories, playing with words, is for me, a way of reaching out beyond my narrow life, reaching out beyond my narrow death—it uncrowds my head, pacifies the ghosts, and [in a very small way] makes my life worth my while. So does fishing & drinking & painting & walking beaches & all other forms of dreaming.[1]

It is blessed and irksome when a writer describes their process and motivations so adroitly. There seems nothing left to say. But because this stretching towards life-meaning is so turbulent, and itself explores most of these 'other forms of dreaming', let's go through Hulme's wordplay anyway.

'Tara Diptych' opens the collection, a Rosetta Stone promising a riot of meaning, premised on the fact that 'there are at least 21 meanings for *tara*', the word that 'sets the whole thing up'. Tara is 'the frame—one marvellous 21-jointed word, full of diversities' and, from its potential, Hulme purports to be 'merely weaver, making senses for the sounds', taking this material to 'weave anew'.

Te Kaihau boasts plenty of misanthrope's games, but 'Swansong' is of a different order. During the Springbok tour protests of 1981, we follow pro-tour agitators plotting gratuitous violence against 'those slimy commie liblips', getting their 'own low jollies' by taking to the protesters with scalpels and tasers. In the garbled vernacular of one of the scalpel-wielding stirrers, it reads like Aotearoa's *A Clockwork Orange*. The droogs go in disguise, with 'stencilled peace signs on the t-shirts' to blend in, 'feeling ready to break the world apart'. Enraged by 'the crowdmass chanting their palsied trendyleft slogans', sickened by the 'scummy bodies' around them, they're itching for their misanthrope's game.

But the misanthropes are themselves being gamed: by a slight, manic pixie who is more than she looks. We feel it sooner than the antagonists do, our unease *just* preceding their own realisation of 'the undertow' of her words ('dangerously sweet and low'), her 'demure smile, little white fangs hidden'. She (the unnamed 'bitch') is a Valkyrie, selector of the slain, conveyor of the dead to Valhalla. Was this all a dream born of concussion, or too much ecstasy, or a real confrontation with the supernatural? Does it matter if we never know?

'A Tally of the Souls of Sheep' is an ovine revenge story against a freezing worker on holiday. A screenplay for a bach horror film, with haunting explanatory notes running alongside the script. Hulme's script annotations are riddles, jokes on the reader, dictionary definitions, a chilling 'phantom voice', and crystalline statements of ethics. Through close-ups—steel hooks being driven through sheep tendons; boning knives and sharpening steels; the housewife's 'macabre sandwich' of kiwifruit and steak—we witness the violence of the abattoir and of domesticity.

'One Whale, Singing' and 'The Knife and The Stone' explore domestic confinement, but also the tools—tangible and intangible—we need to survive. Beyond the illustrative whetstone and gutting knife, we need language, interiority, connection to the non-human. Hulme conjures her own language, forging countless compound words: 'eyejuice', 'slimefroth', 'stainscarred silverstudded caries-scarred grinning'. With a keen ear for aurality, Hulme is a wizard of onomatopoeia, rendering the 'thocketty of chopper wings', and capturing the music of marine life, from the 'gothic sonorific cathedral song' of whales to the 'thin hiss and crackle' of krill. She is also attuned to the rank sounds ('the fleshy slop! slop!' of a man's lips) and fetid smells of human life and decay ('blood-stink, like old menses or meat on the turn'). This is a writer in love with the roll and reel of words, their mouthfeel, their alliterative possibilities, their pulse and play on the paper. Her form, too, becomes whatever she wants, whittling down to prose poems when the mood demands, when it serves the purpose.

Relationships unspool slowly, never giving the reader any sense of omniscience, or even a clear handle on who is what to whom. We learn only incrementally of family trees and enmities. (Indeed, nothing is definitive because 'It all depends / on what story / you hear.') Children and adults pay sustained, intimate attention to natural phenomena, to the creatures crackling all around them. But sometimes that intimacy becomes fatal: Gwen, a child, discovers 'a deep and belly-satisfying side to killing'. Against the rising heat and 'chainsaw racket' of the cicadas, tempers rise, and children slip into sadism. Tragedy always seems close—either imminent or immanent, darkening every doorstep, furrowing every brow.

Even the happiness is manic, the good relationships sour, bodies wake with 'a prescience of pain', marae protocol stings, the children have lost their limbs or been lost to the sea, there is 'a holocaust of krill', the massacre of cicadas, and at a kite-flying party a withdrawn scholar is tempted to 'dive down through any one of their dancing brittle skulls'. Often the narrator is drunk, high, concussed, or all three, issuing booze-fuelled night-scrawls of grief.

I wasn't expecting quite this many sex scenes, but there you go. It's a classic for a reason. We make love in the midst of death, in the bowels of despair. The title story itself features a feathered penis, and 'Tara' is saturated with the sucking and sluicing of lovers, one of Hulme's unspecified forms of dreaming: 'You disturb me he says … the peach juice drips /

he grips a finger pointed to groin / until blood swells it stiff.' This sweet viscosity returns in 'A Window Drunken in the Brain', where the narrator drips peach juice and 'He licks the juice of me, he licks it off. I finish the peach and suck long upon the stone.' Wallow, lick, drip, suck, nipple, ooze, 'those sly teeming nuts in their wrinkled cosy pouch'. Hulme tuts at our open mouths: 'We all know menus that are transports of lust / to love.'

Some material doesn't play so well, almost four decades on. In 'Kaibutsu-San', for example, the condescending phonetic spelling of all dialogue from 'the little Jap', who cannot pronounce the letter 'l' ('O but I ruv cards, prease pray more.') We would not accept this written now, I hope. However, some of Ian Wedde's stories contain this same feature ('Paradise'). Thankfully, this is not the only link between these reissued classics. A thicker, noisier nexus is the thrum of cicadas, which stays in your ear throughout each book.

Another link, figuratively connected to their subterraneous lifespans (cicada nymphs live most of their lives underground, shedding multiple exoskeletons before emerging to the surface) is the phenomenon of characters who prickle their hosts, haunting them for years, for decades, before they are worked from short stories into heaving, whakapapa-rich novels. Simon, of *The Bone People*, is prefigured in 'A Drift in Dream', written years before. In this short story we meet Simon's birth mother (a former nun) and father, a young man rent by grief when she is killed in a car accident.

This is the beginning of Simon's harrowing story, his earliest beatings. As Hulme noted in 1985, 'The characters wouldn't go away. They took 12 years to reach this shape.'² In the small-time industrialist and his nemesis in Wedde's 'The Shirt Factory' we meet an early iteration of the themes and historical figures that populate *The Reed Warbler* (2020), Wedde's generation-spanning novel of emigration and family history.

First published as a collection in 1981, *Dick Seddon's Great Dive and Other Stories* is a bipolar romp through the recent history of Aotearoa. Suicide, isolation, breakdowns, casual violence and drug (ab)use, necrotic relationships that eat away at all parties involved—a buffet of bleak themes that somehow roars with energy and aesthetic pleasures. Character, in these stories, is the pulse that keeps everything going, that sustains the fictional ecology. This pulse is deliberately irregular, a calculated risk. In the 2022 introduction, Wedde recognises his characters as 'deliberately unlikeable', and 'wish[es] them luck in their encounters with tolerant readers in a changed world'.

The title story occupies the bulk of the volume, swelling with earworms or sticky music: snatches of lyric that come into the story again and again, foreshadowing their actual utterance, and then echoing long after the speech act is complete. Fragments of songs and conversations leaven the chapters just as they worm through the characters' minds. 'Dick Seddon's Great Dive' opens with suicide (or does it?), with the downwards spiral of a self-loathing man, knee deep in the Tasman and sick of the voices, 'the cramped bile of energy' that distorted and distanced 'the world and the friends in it'.

He goes unnamed for several chapters, leaving us to reckon only with 'all the angry force in his body', unleashing itself upon itself. She, too, goes unnamed for some time, and we meet as onlookers, peering through a window at someone writing a biography 'with sad precision, the neatness of someone who's determined to see something through'. Her work feels imperative. She describes herself as a murderer because she couldn't stop what happened. To alleviate her guilt, she needs to write his life story. We meet the unhinged and the steadfast, roles that chop and change throughout the text.

They, the star-crossed couple, are Chink and Kate. He, a lush, a user, a womaniser (his motto: 'I'm not dependable'), is described as 'strung out' along the north–south axis, 'stretched tight between those same poles'. '[H]e gets higher and quieter and crazier' the further south they drive, wearing a smile to split logs. This smile becomes a grim augury, 'the grin … opening his head'. We never learn his real name. Refracted by the male gaze, and never seeing herself clearly, Kate doesn't introduce herself properly until chapter 11, even then describing herself 'as though through a man's eyes. (Chink's eyes.)'

Is Chink bipolar, or just torn between islands and their equally torn history? He knows a lot about history. More than most in this period. And he wears the weight of the past. Certain things he values enough 'to keep present, in that weird grab-bag of knowledge he contrived to lug around like Bunyan's Christian burden'. Chink lectures an American about missionaries, colonisation, the Kīngitanga, ancestral waka, Māori creation stories, the tikanga and kawa (protocol) of death.

He knows so much it freaks people out—tourists and tauiwi. But how do you write the life story of a man like Chink ('the teller of parables, the bullshit artist'), someone who sincerely does not want to be known, other than carnally? A maverick, a conman, a sexually violent man … 'deliberately unlikeable' indeed. Kate's task is doomed. She cannot save herself this way. And Wedde knows this, as he leaps from her present to her past, quick as the lightning of memory. What she comes to realise, through this confessional, is that she was never to blame.

In his late twenties, Wedde wrote compellingly about war and its afterlives, the road-tripping, mandy-necking, dexie-popping counterculture, sleepy small-town New Zealand and the confused metropolis of Auckland in the 1970s. He's also a dab hand at long philosophical musings. Through his characters, Wedde waxes theoretical about memory, decision-making at dawn, transcending melancholia, botched intimacies, the nature of language, time, the neural connections that make up 'meaning', and madness.

An astute art critic, Wedde turns this aesthetic eye to his fictional world, receptive to ugliness and beauty, great and small. Norfolk pines stud the coast 'like burnt-out rockets', and parts of a road trip are rendered as turns of the kaleidoscope, with piercing, labile light 'throwing bright fragments into relief: marigolds, geraniums, the beaks and feet of seabirds … green gems at the mountains' throats'. Ekphrastic writing about photography threads through the story, but everyone's mental health is in the foreground and background of every shot, thudding closer to disaster.

Wedde withholds so much: relationships, motives, pasts, names; all are opaque, merely guessed at, until they spill out unevenly, dousing you with content you're unsure how to fit together. Like Hulme, Wedde pretends to no omniscience, assumes no bird's eye view of things. Even descriptions are uncertain—a fence is 'probably creosoted, with what looks like a passion fruit vine', a little boy is 'probably close to tears', a tree is 'probably a kōwhai'. Nothing is a given, every narrative description is challengeable, possibly (probably) wrong. A pallor of instability, matching our romantic leads. His metaphors and similes, too, brook no questioning: Auckland traffic was 'like blood, a small section of a kind of endless reticulation, a maze, a mystery … yes, and if you tried to make sense of it, you'd go crazy.' Question the imagery, the illusory link, and you're headless. You're Chink.

The auxiliary stories also boast extended delusions of grandeur. In 'Snake', for example, Herman Flag is a dishwasher desperate to become a rock'n'roll Hall of Famer. Vertiginous in its pace, scale, and emotion, 'Snake' muses about the Big Questions (salvation, eternity, music) in strong Kiwi slang. In most of these stories, Wedde's favourite mode is the slightly (or very) manic first-person tirade: verbose, prone to lashing out, to grandstanding, relishing their captive audience, 'concentrated with glad fury upon the details of his monologue' ('The River'). But they are not all narrated this way. 'In Clover' sat with me for a long time, such a clever, satirical portrait of a Pākehā writer and his capable wife.

Hulme wanted her words to last, wanted them carved into the landscape, to 'survive the decay of paper and stone'.[3] Gratitude is owed, of course, to the original editors, and to Te Herenga Waka University Press for launching the THW Classics collection, and ensuring that such gems remain in print. But gratitude is also due to Spiral, the feminist publishing collective that saw the gasp-worthy in Hulme; that helped The Bone People see the light of day; and that laboured for years to prioritise Māori women's writing. Such long-vision patronage of New Zealand literature needs to be sustained.

Writing in 1981, Wedde was right that he 'was putting the spade in deeper than he knew at the time'. The longer narrative arcs of historical angst, vanity, misanthropy, mania and nostalgia are still with us. But each of these authors always asks, 'is there more than one way of looking at this?' For Wedde and Hulme, interpretive flux is an ever-present question. Whatever anything means, these classics help us to wonder.

---

1   Keri Hulme, 'Notes towards a reconciliation of torso & head', in Irihapeti Ramsden, Marian Evans & Miriama Evans (eds), Wahine Kaituhi: Women writers of Aotearoa (Spiral, 1985), p. 24.
2   Hulme in Wahine Kaituhi, inner cover.
3   Hulme, 'Notes towards a reconciliation', p. 24.

Laughter and Forgetting
Wendy Parkins

Laughing at the Dark by Barbara Else (Penguin Random House, 2023), 262pp, $37

'Deciding what to tell' when people ask where she comes from is not easy, Barbara Else confesses on the first page of her memoir, *Laughing at the Dark*. The long answer or the short one? she ponders. A peripatetic childhood as a bank manager's daughter provides the immediate context for the challenge presented by stories of origin but there is more at stake than just a list of childhood homes, from Invercargill to Auckland. A long answer would allow a fuller account, rich with immersive detail, in which digression might perhaps occlude depth. A short answer, by contrast, might offer the comfort of concision, thereby avoiding messier complications. Both options come with their own risks and temptations, as every memoirist learns.

In fact, what Else writes on that first page is 'deciding what to tell them *today*', adding a further dimension to her dilemma. Today is the present moment, the starting point for any memoirist looking back over the course of their life experience, a perspective that inevitably reminds us that our present might easily have been very different from where we now find ourselves. But today is also the product of all the contingent bits and bobs that make up a life right at this precise instant: our mood, the weather, what we just saw on social media, what we have on our to-do list.

What we tell people about ourselves today may not be what we might say if we had slept better or if the sun was shining. So how does a memoirist negotiate this ever-shifting perspective, between deep and abiding memories that seem to encapsulate the essence of who we believe ourselves to be, and the dailiness of life, so unfixed and unpredictable that it is difficult to feel secure in judgements or decisions often made on the hoof? 'Who can trust what they remember?' Else writes. Do distant memories really 'contain clues to the sort of person I've become' here and now?

At first glance, of course, the long answer would seem the obvious choice for a memoirist with such a richly rewarded career to look back on as Else. Over more than three decades she has written novels, plays, short stories and poetry, for both adults and children. She has won numerous awards and honours, held prestigious residencies and fellowships, and carried out trail-blazing work as a literary agent and assessor discovering and mentoring New Zealand writers. Such glittering accomplishments, though, might never have been possible if she had remained in her first marriage, so Else's story is also representative of its time: a familiar story, but no less important for that reason, of the significant changes in the roles and opportunities available to New Zealand women in the second half of the twentieth century.

What ultimately prompts this memoir, however, is the impact of a cancer diagnosis, the kind of searing life event that has the capacity to up-end all certainties and future plans, requiring an urgent reassessment of everything, colouring whatever we thought we knew.

So Else begins with her first memory, the source of her memoir's title:

> I must be less than two years old (I remember the nappy), standing in a kitchen cupboard that reaches from the bench right to the ceiling. My father keeps shutting the door, opening, shutting. Each time it opens I explode into laughter.

This golden moment of childhood shared with a kind and playful father reminds Else, in turn, of her mother always saying 'Look on the funny side,' which perhaps provides the key to interpreting this memory. 'Laughing helps to keep things under control,' Else concludes, and thus brings into play a rather different meaning. Laughter can be life-affirming and unguarded but it can also be a deliberate defence against acknowledging what is much harder to say or think or even feel. Light and darkness, laughter and (a willed) forgetting. Else's story, as it unfolds, will weave skilfully back and forth between the two, framed by an ongoing account of the rigours of her cancer treatment in the present.

Growing up female at a time when it was becoming possible to pursue personal freedoms while still subjected to double standards about achievement meant that marriage and motherhood remained the expected outcome for the young Barbara. Her male peers at university never needed to question their ambitions but for women it was different. It is shocking to be reminded how comparatively recent it was that even postgraduate study might be seen as over-reaching for a woman, whatever her grades or talents.

Here, as throughout, Else captures the ambivalence of her feelings about this situation in a clear-eyed manner that is often funny and never self-indulgent. As the young wife of a rising academic physician moving from one research institute to another, she performs her socially prescribed role with good grace, while noticing acerbically the foibles and failings of the characters she meets. Else's powers of observation are a frequent source of humour, even while her narrative makes painfully clear how hard she was working to stave off the kind of self-knowledge that might upset the comfortable continuities of family life. But self-deception can only last so long and the story of the unravelling of her first marriage is told with courageous candour.

Alongside the story of her second marriage, to fellow writer Chris Else, Barbara then describes the blossoming of her writing career, from tentative beginnings to early success, consolidation and reward. The exploration of the writing process in this second half of the memoir is particularly absorbing and I would have liked to see more space devoted to Else's frank discussions of the precarious early stages of new projects, rather than the overly episodic events calendar of literary festivals, workshops and invitations (although the Bryce Courtenay anecdote was well worth the setup). It is perhaps unfortunate that struggle makes a better story than success, if only because the dramatic momentum of overcoming adversity holds the reader in a way that the stasis of achievement cannot, so when Else begins to wrestle with her emerging impulse to write a memoir it felt that more was at stake once again.

Earliest memories, Else writes, 'might get you writing' but:

> they're not enough to create story propulsion. Because a memoir isn't an autobiography, not a detailed listing of every darn thing. Doesn't a memoir have to be about something more than—I don't know—more than the person? To have a focus on … what? Isn't it a personal search for …?

Her use of ellipses here captures Else's doubts and prevarications—does her life have enough drama for a memoir?—while also signalling a refreshing honesty about the fraught project of memoir writing, whereby self is the focus but not the goal. Paradoxically, in writing about what is most personal, most private, memoir has the potential to take both author and reader to an outcome or a kind of knowledge that the memoirist didn't have at the start of the project—if they are willing to go there.

Else concludes this chapter, 'So I am not going to do a memoir,' but we know this is not the end of the story and soon she describes returning to her memoir, having settled on the simple aim to 'show what happened', to show 'how the tiny detail or moment shocks or illuminates'. As with so many writing projects over the past few years, however, global events then intervene, but to be alive is always to be in the midst of mortality; the pandemic is the personal too.

For a writer, that means putting down on paper the ellipses and the question marks, accepting doubt and uncertainty, but carrying on writing anyway. This is what Else ultimately does, despite the odds and thanks to an unexpected medical reprieve. Describing all that she has achieved thus far in a manner that is somehow both modest and unapologetic, Else also gives us a personal story of loss and love that is generously peopled with family, friends and community.

It was a pity, though, to see a number of editorial errors slip through in the work of such a distinguished writer. For example, the names of authors J.M. Barrie and Eleanor Dark are both misspelled, and the monumental rock formation in Katoomba, Australia, is mistakenly called The Seven Sisters, four siblings too many.

A Family Story

Helen Watson White

Always Going Home—Lauris and Frances Edmond: A mother and daughter story by Frances Edmond (Otago University Press, 2022), 292pp, $40

'As a Pākehā New Zealander,' writes the late Frances Edmond in *Always Going Home*, 'I am aware of the nourishing and sustaining power of whakapapa, even a little envious of it.' In her unusually compelling book, finished during the author's last illness, Frances has enlarged upon the legacy of her mother, poet Lauris Edmond, by combining insights the two women had int o their late twentieth-century times. In pursuing her own whakapapa, Frances explains why she finds history fascinating: 'It gives me a sense of my location in the world, both immediate and distant. 'Not exactly "knowing one's place" in the social and economic hierarchies—though that's part of it—more one's heritage; a sense of belonging.'

One of Edmond's key threads is that poet-mother and actor-daughter have felt, even through times of painful disagreement, that they belonged together. In what is a fairly complicated family/literary story, the two seemed to be on the same plane, as feminist sisters, or best friends. Frances Edmond's 'personal narrative' has been written in the years after Lauris died, quoting from their many letters to each other and the diaries Lauris kept all her life, until her death in early 2000.

The letter-writing continued the habit established by Lauris's correspondence with her own mother, Fanny Scott, which formed the basis of *Hot October* (1989), the first of three volumes of Lauris's autobiography. The second volume, *Bonfires in the Rain* (1991), begins with Fanny's letters to her children, marking a new stage in the parents' lives when they took their first trip abroad. There's a parallel here: the movement of Lauris's story that Frances tells (although not chronologically) is from a mother's first connections with her children, in the setting of a traditional family, to her breaking out of her marriage into the life of a writer, with all the disruption that entailed. Lauris's was a life in two halves, as Frances remarks, her mother calling her education and child-rearing years 'life number one'. Her second life involved acting upon longheld literary aspirations while retaining the sense of home and family that informed her writing from the start.

In the book's first section, 'Origins', Frances juxtaposes two stories about the competing claims of life and art. Lauris's poem about her grandmother Clara Eliza tells of a 13-year-old becoming the family housekeeper when her stepmother died, then marrying at 17 and bearing 12 children, raising them with 'imagination' and love. No divided life there, as Lauris wrote: 'August little lady, you used / every second of your dense half century creating / a clan …' Later Frances describes Lauris's 'surprised and continuing delight' in her role of grandmother. When her first grandchild was born in 1977, Lauris was on PEN writers' business in Czechoslovakia, the news coming to her by telegram to New Zealand House in London. Frances quotes her mother's response from *The Quick World*, the third part of her autobiography: 'The fact that my closest attention was every day fixed on my literary occupations, rather than my old domestic ones, was beside the point. Life, not art, would always sweep in and grab the prizes.' Frances remarks, 'This is a theme—a conflict—to which she would regularly return and never completely resolve.'

Frances turns from describing the exacting conditions of life for Clara to recalling her mother's domestic near-servitude two generations later. In the dimly lit wash-house at home in Ohakune a child watches the laundry being done: 'our clothes agitating in greyish water in the green machine or being caught in wet bundles on the end of a stick and shoved through the ringer, flopping down flattened into the cold rinsing water in the concrete tubs on either side'.

Sensory memories like this put flesh on the bones of the genealogical table at the end of the book, which shows Lauris and Trevor's six children arriving over 11 years (Virginia in 1948, Frances 1950, Martin 1952, Rachel 1954, Stephanie 1957, and Katherine 1959). From 1977 to 1999, as 15 grandchildren entered the world, Lauris would 'write a poem and/or dedicate a book, to the latest addition'. She was, records Frances,

> ever present in my family life—letters and visits, faxes and phone calls, books she made by hand for each of my children, rugs knitted for their beds, presents at Easters, birthdays, Christmases and other occasions when no festive excuse was in evidence, just a desire to connect ... I used to wonder when she found time to do any work.

Clara, who bore twice as many children, lived to only about 53 years and Lauris to 75. Indeed, it was only after she turned 50 that Edmond came into her own as a writer, publishing her first volume of poems, *In Middle Air*, in 1975. But 'life number one' and 'life number two' were not sequential, Frances wrote, 'continuing to cross over and sometimes blend'. For some years, too, Lauris and Frances were experiencing the 'tension' between work and family at the same time. There was also, of course, tension between them. Frances bemoans the fact that while her mother was staying with her in Auckland, when she could have done with some help at home, Lauris instead was 'gallivanting' about the city on her own affairs.

Frances describes her mother's journey as 'drawn out, messy, agonising', knowing that Lauris lived the full complexity of a divided life with no role models. By convention, 'life number one' had rendered the person invisible—or worse, the target of a belittling cast of mind, which was considered normal at the time. Consequently, Frances easily absorbed the view that her mother's theatrical activities were marginal while her father's similar pursuits 'took centre stage'.

Her mother gave her main energy to keeping the family going, but even that role could be marginalised. Frances quotes the diary passage in *Bonfires in the*

Rain where Lauris pinpoints the moment she recognised, 'with blinding clarity', the gulf between herself and her family:

> I didn't exist, except as I helped them to exist. Without them I was nothing, and so they perceived me—theirs, useful, indeed necessary, loved, of course, depended upon; but as a person with possible separate requirements of my own, not there. And nobody, not even I, thought this unbalanced or wrong.

The sort of existential alienation she describes reminds me of the tenor of Janet Frame's autobiography.

There are other considerations, however, unique to this book. The daughter story, while it amounts to Frances's autobiography, also presents Lauris's pre-1975 life through a daughterly lens. But Frances's retrospective observations carry more freight. By the time she comes to write the two-sided story she is herself a mother, with empathy for Lauris's trials, particularly through the children's teenage years, when 'tumult and pandemonium were common in our large and disparate household'. The section titled 'Daughter to Mother: The wheel turns' is headed by lines from a Lauris villanelle:

> A mother's love is bred into the bone.
> A daughter wants her life to be her own.

Lauris's relationships with her five daughters evolved, we are told, from 'passionate beginnings and sacrifices' through 'intense intimacies' to 'sobering hard-won self-knowledge'. But this was no simple, linear progression. Frances reveals, for instance, that her mother's need for a confidante upset her 17-year-old self. She would 'resist coming home', in case Lauris was 'in a state' and wanting to pour out her marital woes. Yet when Frances left for university, she relied on her mother's loving support and wrote copious letters home: 'outpourings of angst and excitement, embarrassment and joie de vivre ... new ideas and ways of thinking and being' such as Lauris had written to her mother too.

The Frances of these letters, sensing and responding to everything with a fierce attention, is still evident when she comes to treat life-happenings of a different kind. There is an acutely personal quality to her narrative of the year 1975, when her younger sister Rachel died by suicide. Frances's account of this 'potent psychic event in the family' is preceded by a description of her childhood in the 'rough, wild landscape' of Ohakune. Her lament for that life which is 'irretrievably passed' becomes conjoined to her grief at the loss of Rachel, who shared the near-idyll of life in the country before falling victim to sexual violence elsewhere. Rachel's mental illness, closely experienced by Frances, her parents and siblings, is described in its raw exactness, Lauris's diary entry included for its poignant picture of Rachel's expression in death: 'A look of age and suffering comprehension of far more than any young girl should know or have to know.'

In Lauris's diaries, Frances had a bank of material showing her mother grappling with the issues of her lives, her loves and her art. But she doesn't overuse that resource, preferring rather to quote from poems, for Lauris transmuted everything of her life into her work. The book progressively reveals how being present—a state only possible after Lauris had her 'epiphany'—became an essential condition for writing poetry, as for engaging with others. At times, indeed, Lauris was accused of being *too* present for some in the family, and also of using their lives as subject matter. Frances canvasses the range of situations where emotional boundaries were transgressed, herself having to judge the appropriateness of what she might include.

The author mainly wants us to understand: she helps us interpret, for instance, the photographs she has chosen to represent different states of being present, in Lauris's story. While a family group snapped in Ohakune in 1956 shows her 32-year-old mother slightly removed, 'tired, wistful', possibly pregnant for the fifth time, another photo from 1964, with the full complement of smiling children, presents the parents as more relaxed, settling into their roles. Was this the peak of their achievement, perhaps, in society's eyes?

Against that image of an ideal nuclear family we are led to compare Lauris's hard-won independence: going back to university in middle age, falling in love with a succession of men; travelling to Menton to take up the Mansfield Fellowship in 1981, or to London in 1985 to receive the Commonwealth Poetry prize. Frances's searching and respectful text provides what no two-dimensional image could convey: the agony of her mother's slow separation from her father—even while they inhabited the same house—through his repeated mental breakdowns and the loss of his career; and Lauris's earnest attempts to bring the family together when many close bonds had been severed, even if sometimes reformed, only to break again.

There is despair in this interwoven story but there's also inspiration—lots of it. Through all the cross-currents of their private and public lives there was clearly a partnership between Lauris and Frances. When Frances graduated from Toi Whakaari/New Zealand Drama School in 1975, mother and daughter worked side by side at both life and art. Although Frances rejected the idea of writing a formal literary biography, she was her mother's literary executor, having read or performed, recorded and given feedback on a great deal of her work. The book shows how she developed an intimate knowledge of Lauris's poems and the background to their composition, first while Lauris was alive to share them, then more recently through putting together her mother's last poetry volume, *Late Song*, and co-editing *Night Burns with a White Fire: The essential Lauris Edmond*, both books being published posthumously.

We are shown 25 years of mature collaborations, the pair co-managing readings in person and on radio, and working together on a solo play, *Between Night and Morning*, which Lauris wrote for Frances to perform. Both became confident artists in their different fields, appreciating each other's gifts and furthering each other's influence. Frances Edmond's achievement in this vividly written story is testament to their artistry and their love.

The Poetic Breath
John Geraets

Face to the Sky by Michele Leggott (Auckland University Press, 2022), 92pp, $35; **Letter to 'Oumuamua** by James Norcliffe (Otago University Press, 2023), 96pp, $25; **A Lack of Good Sons** by Jake Arthur (Te Herenga Waka University Press, 2023), 76pp, $25

Required in this review to address three poetry books, I have assigned each book a separate corner within an equilateral triangle, allowing me to speak about their distinctiveness within a shared perimeter of poetic practice.

Typically, individual poetry volumes in this country are A5 in size (especially university publications), sporting a mildly suggestive, two-tone front cover, and a fulsome blurb and pic of the poet at the back. The 100-odd white pages within are covered in *exclusively* black type, comprising around 50 individual titles.[1]

This straightforward setup, bolstered by a detailing of source materials and personal acknowledgements, serves to highlight the book's imaginative contents. The link to imagination remains pivotal. A clear instance is Michele Leggott's evocative poem 'Neinei in blossom at Mokau', which is seen to grow out of the accompanying note: 'The Alexander Turnbull Library in Wellington holds Emily Harris's watercolour of red neinei inscribed "Mokau, Jan 1890".'[2]

And, indeed, it is Leggott, doyenne—one is tempted to say kuia[3]—of our poetry, whom I place at the apex of the triangle, given the acumen on display in this, her eleventh collection. Her male compatriots, occupying the two base angles, are unlike her and each other. Avuncular James Norcliffe, another seasoned practitioner with 11 volumes, reflects on everyday human quandaries in verse and prose, as does a spryer Jake Arthur, who has produced his first book. Jacobean in temperament (a Renaissance scholar), Arthur's verses are conventionally shaped and his acerbic wit is pin-sharp.

Face to the Sky, the title of Leggott's collection, extends for her a longstanding visual motif that has profound importance in terms of concrete observations, either personally experienced or recorded by others, and in developing an *in-seeing* capability through which these are transformed into 'angelic life' (epigraph, Escher). The process invites an ornate phraseology: 'intercochlear space', 'phosphorescent medusae', 'angelic life dialogue wonder', 'beautifully luminous', 'mezzaluna rocking', 'between worlds and mirror light'. While Leggott's encroaching blindness—due to a retinitis pigmentosa condition—has necessitated an increasing reliance on assistance from others, it has also served as a springboard to personal renovation and a celebration of communitarian artistic endeavour.[4]

Just as 'Haemopoiesis' beautifully captures the inner distress caused by 'a transformative but ultimately unsuccessful stem cell transplant' for a cancer condition ('a new body and a new soul'), 'Walks and days' is a poem that shares a panorama of acquaintants and immediate family members in a range of adventures, by turn painful and liberating. A critical point is the collapse and subsequent death on the 'spiral road / on the white shell path' leading down from the Maungauika summit (in the Leggott neighbourhood) of beloved guide-dog Olive ('we have killed our dog'). Another is the 'how many stories can you trust' statement of allegiance to the poet's similarly beloved artist mother:

> the reviewer went looking online for the paintings attributed to my mother
> they weren't there because I invented them both
> and made my mother an artist of the floating world
> would she have liked what I have done impossible to say
> but she would have recognised each detail because I drew them all from our life together in that house on the hill at Urenui

Verisimilitude has a binary aspect (intimated in the repetition of 'wingbeat | featherfall' in 'Konene | Wayfarers') whereby factness *becomes* imaginative. Connection between the two resides in an ability to aesthetically pilot otherwise unbridgeable separations: 'here from there us from them / now from then', culminating in: 'I am myself on the other side of nowhere' ('Very fine lace knitting'). And the far-seeing company identified with is that of modernist creative artists and family members past and present, especially Leggott's parents and the nineteenth-century pioneer forebears, Aunt Emily and the great-grandparents who travelled on the later-shipwrecked steamer SS *Gairloch*.

Balancing Leggott's imaginative uplift, I place the comparable downdraught of the two male poets. Norcliffe delineates human foibles, past and present, homely and estranging: '3 a.m.', 'Pink aspirin for the heart', '5.02 from St Pancras', 'Mensuration', 'The body in the bed', 'Life after the Diamond Harbour ferry'. It is an endearing world characterised by a sense of consequential inconsequence, finely observed, appealing through word play and genial humour, albeit inclining at times to the lugubrious:

> And so begins the endless debate about directions and whether this path or that path through the storied suburbs of the past would have been better. This followed by the debate about whether the debate itself has any point.
> ('Insomnia')

The predominant tone is one of affectionate resignation ('We just can't help ourselves', 'But it is too late', 'Part of us wants to believe it'):

> Our tree, of course, and our figs.
> Our wax-eyes, too, we like to claim
> as if they owed us a living or something.
> ('Greenfinches and wax-eyes among the figs')

A keener riposte is evident in the work of Arthur. These are cerebral poems of occasional blood-sport: 'There is a spot on you', 'Styx', 'Dazed panic', 'Drying my sweat cold', 'Lips cold with sweat', 'I was so angry I ate my son'. Unlike Norcliffe, whose protagonists feel unthreatening and familiar, Arthur's, including those referred to as father mother brother lover boyfriend girlfriend, occupy an afflicted atmosphere. It's as if the stanzaic forms are a way of fending off or containing distress, including introspective angst:

> Among the mosaics and trickling water,
> I ask myself if I am a boring person.
> Sometimes I think I may never again
> have an interesting thing to say.
> This is an obstacle to you loving me.
> ('You and the view')

Poems like 'Call time' and 'Hand-eye coordination' ('She wants him sometime in the next now') display a taut syllogistic astuteness, while the sweep of '1588' is deft ('There is a sameness in everything'). 'Spear' is immediately appealing:

> I want to float out of my mind and into my body.
> The body is better.
> With a body, I could draw him in for a kiss.
> With a mind, I could only stop myself doing that.

★

Let me return briefly to the shared perimeter of our equilateral triangle to speak about poetic subjectivity and poetry's valorising purpose.

All three books frequently reference 'I' as the axis about which 'real world' events are refigured. Despite plentiful they-you-we-he-she markers of otherness, the books abide in the voice of the speaker, through which the poetry, as much as it endeavours to respect the usual constraints of time and place, supersedes them.[5] Around the axis of poetic subjectivity run the circle-like processes of existence, for which 'I' is centripetal.[6] In this way, the revered tradition in which the poet speaks in tongues is perpetuated. Just as the poetic breath becomes *another* (inhale inspiration exhale transformation), the world depicted transcends the one recorded.

For Leggott, this is personified in communitarian artistic endeavour;[7] for Norcliffe, a shoring against desuetude ('We lived within careful / Parameters and had / Circumscribed extremes' ('Living in the Goldilocks Zone'); for Arthur, it entails contestation within the contemporary 'scene', among customs and costumes, between artfulness and awfulness, vacuity and enormity ('I would look at a million designs / and die having chosen nothing', 'Hark').

The misgiving I have about such a renovative poetics is its continuing to see as irreproachable poetic subjectivity's rendering of time and place in its own image. The difficulty in equating the voice of subjectivity with truthful revelation is that the former subsumes the latter and becomes—however notionally, however briefly—the ruler of the (real) world. This is hardly a solution to the world's ills, should such be poetry's aim.

---

[1] All three appear from university presses, as do, at least in part, two of our major still-paper literary magazines, Landfall and Poetry Aotearoa Yearbook.

[2] Artist-poet Emily Harris is 'the sister of my great-great-grandfather' (Notes, Mezzaluna: Selected Poems). Ancestors figure prominently as dramatic personae and touchstones of value in Leggott's later poetry.

3   The claim feels culturally and ethnically precocious, although several Leggott poems assume bilingual titles and, since 2007–09, when she was poet laureate, increasing dollops of te reo Māori appear in her work.

4   Poems recount historical events in a way that uplifts them into the extensive imaginative present. For example, the infant death of emigrant Sarah's fourth child en route to New Zealand is spoken of 'as an active presence' (Note, 'I have named her Amelia'). The very next note directly addresses Leggott's poetic enquiry into 'family memory': 'What can be recovered? What is beyond reach of the written or remembered record?' 'What's behind language if you pierce it full of holes / what is nothing when it comes around twice / we have the fragments now for the connections', enquires 'Walks and days'.

5   Leggott's historicity, Norcliffe's everyday fabulae (like the funeral director whom his wife—and subsequently his poem— amusingly abbreviates as 'Fun Dr'), and Arthur's intense (usually unnamed) dramatic personae, occupy a range of times and places.

6   'And when I asked him, "Frank [O'Hara]," one time I said on the telephone, "why is it that we keep writing poems?" he said "well, have you ever read any that have already been written?"' (Anne Waldman, 'Excerpt from an interview with Kenneth Koch, New York City', 1980): http://jacketmagazine.com/15/koch-waldman.html

7   'In the 1960s my family came to live in Carrington St in New Plymouth, unaware of the intricately layered history that underlies each step on the road passing by outside' (Note, 'The wedding party'). 'The body of the poem consists of quotations from nineteenth-century newspaper reports of the first Taranaki war' (Note, 'Speaking distance').

You Put Your Whole Self In, You Put Your Whole Self Out

Iain Sharp

Say I Do This: Poems 2018–2022 by C.K. Stead (Auckland University Press, 2023), 108pp, $35; **Respirator: A Poet Laureate collection 2019–2022** by David Eggleton (Otago University Press, 2023), 192pp, $35

In my early teens I used to go to the Saturday morning sessions at the Onehunga skating rink. The programme was always the same, and the part I liked most called for all the young skaters to form a big circle and attempt the 'Hokey Cokey' on wheels: 'You put your whole self in / You put your whole self out / You put your whole self in / And you shake it all about.'

The 'Hokey Cokey', and notions of putting one's self in, or leaving it out, came back to me while reading the latest collections from two of our recent poets laureate. In *Say I Do This*, C.K. Stead attempts few new tricks but he reprises old favourites—updated versions of Horace and Catullus, psalms of Judas, Baxterian sonnets, tercets of varying line length—with a suave grace and an expert control of tone. The sheer heft of David Eggleton's *Respirator* suggests that the last five years have been the most fecund of his never-idle career. Each of the seven sections is distinct enough in mood and method to be considered a separate chapbook.

Reading these poets together, however, sharpens awareness of their differences. Stead is firmly within the egocentric post-Romantic tradition. His experiences and opinions are at the core of his poetry. Even when he adopts the guise of Horace, Catullus or Judas, the mask is loosely attached and semi-transparent, so we can discern C.K.'s features behind it. Moreover, the first-person voice heard throughout *Say I Do This* is pretty much identical with the 'C.K. Stead' who addresses us in his critical essays and three volumes of autobiography.

Indeed, so closely intertwined are Stead's verse and life that the autobiography is useful for identifying people mentioned in the new poems. Those curious about Stead's 'first true love Diane (pronounced as in French)', for example, should read the fifteenth and sixteenth chapters of *South-West of Eden: A Memoir 1932–1956*, and those intrigued by 'our friend Bill', the extravagant hero of 'The Money', who loses more than one fortune and whose first wife was 'a Mary Quant model', should read pages 407–09 of *What You Made of It: A Memoir 1987–2020*.

David Eggleton, on the other hand, for all his street-savvy rock 'n' roll trappings, can seem at times a throwback to the pre-Romantic era when poets seldom mentioned their personal circumstances but instead presented essays in rhyming couplets about the vanity of human wishes. True, in recent interviews he has been forthcoming about his Rotuman heritage and in June 2021 he wrote in some detail about his upbringing in Fiji and South Auckland for the Pacific Arts Legacy Project. But while Eggleton's Pasifika background no doubt feeds into his poetry—in the awareness of the lasting damage done by colonisation, the distrust of politicians of all hues, the scornful disregard for 'squillionaires'—he rarely makes his own experiences the central subject matter of his poems. There are no fond reminiscences of boyhood adventures, adolescent amours, overseas trips, radiant moments, pals both living and deceased—Stead's poetic stock-in-trade. He would rather disappear into a tricky persona: one of Captain Cook's killers, a reborn Dante Alighieri 'mov[ing] in a mall coma', a humpback whale, Donald Trump.

'It's all about dave,' Eggleton tells us, tongue in cheek, in 'Too Many Daves', a fascinating poem in *Respirator*'s final section. Perhaps from the author's perspective it all, obliquely, is. But the poem as 'selfie' has never been to his taste.

As a long-time reader of Stead, I know (because he tells us) the names of his wife, children, parents, sisters, widowed grandmother, boyhood pals, early girlfriends, mentors, rivals, colleagues, even one of the family cats (Zac the Knife). I can likewise recite (again, because he tells us) the street addresses of places with special significance for him: his childhood home (67 Kensington Avenue, Mt Eden), his residence for the past 60 years (37 Tohunga Crescent, Parnell), the home of his friend and mentor Allen Curnow (across the road and up the hill at 62 Tohunga Crescent) and the fibrolite bach of his other 'miglior fabbro' Frank Sargeson (14 Esmond Road, Takapuna, where Janet Frame also dwelled in 1955, a year regarded by Stead as an 'annus mirabilis'). All of these addresses and many of the familiar personnel appear in Say I Do This.

By contrast, all I know about Eggleton from Respirator is that he lives in Dunedin, but we're not told which vicinity, let alone which street. The second section of the book is titled 'Rāhui: Lockdown Journal', but the 'journal' functions far more as a public record than a private diary. He has fun at the expense of public figures (presenting Jacinda Ardern as a hippie 'primmer's teacher' and having Ashley Bloomfield's 'voice of pragmatic calm' give way to 'a Dalek's krark krark'). But we never discover who else, if anyone, is part of Eggleton's household (or 'bubble', as we were briefly taught to say).

The best description of Eggleton's modus operandi that I know is the back-cover blurb for his 1995 collection Empty Orchestra: 'some poems were not so much written as assembled: questioning, promiscuous postmodern collages. They are all made out of language found here in Aotearoa/New Zealand and recycled into a poetic record of what's been happening in the immediate past, by an eyewitness and participant'. Twenty-eight years later, some tweaking is needed. Eggleton's grasp of the past now extends beyond the immediate to take in the last few centuries and his zone of interest has broadened beyond Aotearoa to encompass all of the South Pacific. The fifth section of Respirator, 'The Death of Kapene Kuke', is set in Hawaii, with Honolulu seen as the epicentre for how a once-thriving Polynesian culture can be despoiled by capitalist greed.

At heart, though, Eggleton remains a promiscuous collagist, more eyewitness than 'I', seizing magpie-like on any sound-bite that takes his fancy, whether belligerent bogan ('get a gorse bush up yah'), Pasifika bro-speak ('Howzit braddah whale'), Covid talk ('superspreaders', 'clusters', 'airborne droplets', 'strict sanitation', 'Level Four' etc), or inane radio chatter ('I'll tell you what matters, / what really really matters. / What really matters, / that's what matters'). Had he not recoiled at an early age from academia with its 'atmosphere of self-congratulatory Masonic handshakes', Eggleton might have become a distinguished professor of sociolinguistics.

While reading Respirator, I also found helpful this sentence from Eggleton's 2006 publication Into the Light: A history of New Zealand photography: 'Like a protest placard, the nature photograph warns us to save the wilderness and, like a communal hymn, exhorts us to share the photographer's reverence.' The note of urgent protest is clear in the parts of Respirator where Eggleton doom-scrolls the landscape, detecting rusted bed-springs in the landfill, bulging black trash bags, brownish rivers, earthquake damage, vape fug, tractor tyre marks and so forth. Yet Eggleton's reverential regard for natural beauty is also present throughout the book; take, for instance, these luminous lines from the 'Lockdown Journal':

> Oh to sail like a falcon over Franz Josef,
> its bluey-white ice, to the grizzled silver
> of braided rivers in their mournfulness,
> coasting leeward of the Alps, one more time.

What is unusual about Eggleton is the ease with which he can switch register from the psalm-like to rocking razzmatazz. As well as a history of New Zealand photography, he has written a history of New Zealand rock music, *Ready to Fly* (2003). Popular music has always been important to him, serving as a kind of alternative canon to the literary classics. With his penchant for street language and zany quick-fire rhymes, his verse is often closer in texture to rock lyrics than to the book-based pantheon. Parts of *Respirator* transported me back to my roller-skating teenage self, who was yet to discover most printed poetry, but who loved the exuberant wordplay of Bob Dylan and other rockers, without demanding much structural rigour from them, content just to let favourite lines fizz and zing in my head.

Here, from a welter of possibilities, are a few of Eggleton's zingers: 'We waltzed by the coin-in-slot waterfall', 'I raged like a loon beneath a hideous moon', 'full as a bull, bellowing and randy / looking for a share of hashmagandy', 'I enter the centre / to dissent from my mentor', 'just press the button, bro, and up we all go'.

As a laureate and former *Landfall* editor, supported by the publishing arm of the country's oldest university, Eggleton could hardly be more firmly ensconced in Aotearoa's literary firmament. Yet he still projects a maverick aura. His mischievous side ('tee hee dave', to quote again from 'Too Many Daves') is to the fore in *Respirator*'s sixth section (wittily titled 'Old School Ties'), where he has fun at the expense of New Zealand's literary history in such poems as 'Sargeson Towers' and 'The Great New Zealand Novel'. While Hone Tuwhare is recalled in this section with an affectionate cheek that would have tickled Tuwhare himself ('poet of jugs of amber in the arvo'), a more hostile hyperbole takes over when C.K. Stead is the focus: 'The drive-by, take-down guy, with silver hatchets / and bloody scalps stacked in his trophy cabinet.'

Those nursing wounds from encounters with Stead will no doubt nod their assent. In fairness, though, I must report there's nary a glimpse of the scalp-collecting assassin in *Say I Do This*. Stead is at his most convivial and least battle-prone throughout. The salutes to fellow poets—Kevin Ireland, Fleur Adcock, Tony Rudolf, Sam Hunt, Anthony Thwaite—are among the warmest and least rivalrous he has written and the love poem to his wife, with which he concludes the book, is beautifully heartfelt and direct.

An Ancient Mariner-like theme of 'lov[ing] well both man and bird and beast' ripples through this collection too. In 'Something to tell', Stead rescues a thrush from the family cat and is then disappointed to find himself alone in the house. While a family member, neighbour or visiting pal would do, one suspects that what the old non-believer would like an all-seeing record-keeping deity to award him a gold star for good conduct. It's not that his long-held atheism has diluted into shoulder-shrugging agnosticism in his closing years. 'There is no Next, / that next is Nothing,' he assures us in 'What Next?'. But he understands (because he shares) the human yearnings that lead to religious sentiment in the first place, such as the desire for the personalities one has cherished to somehow persist beyond death.

Stead divides *Say I Do This* into three parts: 'Home', 'Away', '… and Friends'. Given her public quarrels with Stead, eyebrows will be raised at the inclusion of Keri Hulme in the 'Friends' section, and I can imagine Hulme's indignant ghost struggling to wriggle free from the comradely embrace. Stead has always maintained, however, that he feels no animosity towards her. Rather, I think, he is fascinated by her otherness, by a life and career so different from his own, the solitary 'neuter' existence on a remote part of the coastline, the early international success that failed to generate a shelf-load of subsequent works.

For me, mysterious weeping 'Freddy', the hero of 'An encounter in Belsize Park Gardens', is an even more remarkable inclusion in the 'Friends' section than Hulme. This Indian physicist, who once worked in Einstein's Princeton laboratory, has lived in the plush London suburb for 'thirty-five bloody years' but so invisibly that he has begun to doubt his own existence. Hailing from a continent that Stead has not explored and engaged in a field of scholarship with which he is unfamiliar, 'Freddy' seems to symbolise the unknown and neglected—everything, really, that Stead's oeuvre has not elsewhere touched upon.

Most of Stead's books radiate a confidence that all things will become clear when subjected to the author's formidable intellect. *Say I Do This* introduces a note of humility, suggesting that there are things that will elude even the finest minds and at the close of a long and productive life some mysteries will remain. 'Mary', the longest poem in the 'Home' section, is a quietly moving elegy to Stead's next-door neighbour. Although he was acquainted with this unassuming woman for nearly 60 years, at the end he knew next to nothing about her inner life. The unknown—and perhaps unknowable—can be as close as the backyard fence.

Without the prompting of this review, I doubt if I would have read Stead and Eggleton in tandem, but I am grateful for the experience and would recommend it to others as a kind of masterclass in poetic strategies. David Eggleton takes his title from the metaphor of poetry as a life-support system, implying that for the poet rendering the world into words is as essential as breathing. Karl Stead, I'm sure, would broadly agree. But that still leaves plenty of questions to examine. Which parts of the multifarious world are most worth rendering? Into which words in which patterns? And, of course, where to position the self?

UNITY BOOKS

57 Willis Street, Wellington | 19 High St, Auckland
04 499 4245 | 09 307 0731
wellington@unitybooks.co.nz | auckland@unitybooks.co.nz
www.unitybooksonline.co.nz

There's reading for all tastes at...

Telling TALES
Scorpio Children's Books

Christchurch Central City
ph. 03 741 3309
scorpiobooks.co.nz/tellingtales

ŌTEPOTI – HE PUNA AUAHA

DUNEDIN UNESCO
CITY OF LITERATURE

www.cityofliterature.co.nz

NEW FROM OTAGO UNIVERSITY PRESS

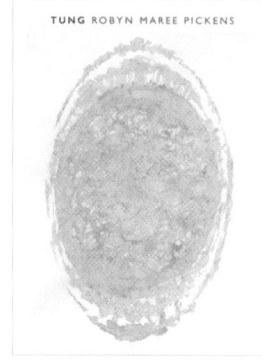

Tung
By Robyn Maree Pickens
ISBN 9781990048609
Paperback, $25

At the Point of Seeing
By Megan Kitching
ISBN 9781990048562
Paperback, $25

When I Reach for Your Pulse
By Rushi Vyas
ISBN 9781990048616
Paperback, $25

Robert Lord Diaries
Edited by Chris Brickell,
Vanessa Manhire and Nonnita Rees
ISBN 9781990048586
Paperback, $45

OTAGO UNIVERSITY PRESS
Find our books in all good bookstores
Visit us at oup.nz

GOLD MEDAL
Readers' Favorite
2023 International
Book Awards

"Exits has profoundly impacted the literary world"

— Midwest Book Review

"Pollock's poetry is brilliant"

— Kristiana Reed, editor in chief of Free Verse Revolution

"Dedicated to the beauty and frailty of life, Exits exemplifies the musicality of language."

— Foreword-Clarion Reviews

"Full of wit, insight and provocative imagery, Exits is a masterful collection. The formal poems are the best. Some are sonnets as artful as any by Shakespeare."

— IndieReader, ★★★★★

EXITSPOETRY.NET

VOLUME EDITIONS 2023

I, OBJECT Stella Chrysostomou
SOME THINGS WRONG Thomas Pors Koed

VOLUME.NZ
books@volume.nz

The Landfall Essay Competition 2024

THE LANDFALL ESSAY COMPETITION seeks to encourage Aotearoa writers to continue the tradition of vivid, contentious and creative essay writing.

ENTRIES will be judged by *Landfall* editor Lynley Edmeades and the winner will receive $3000 and a year's subscription to *Landfall*. The winning essay will be published in *Landfall 248*. Entries also have the chance of publication in *Strong Words: The best of the Landfall Essay Competition*.

RECENT COMPETITION WINNERS INCLUDE Siobhan Harvey, Tina Makereti, Andrew Dean, A.M. McKinnon, Tobias Buck, Nina Mingya Powles, Alice Miller, Laurence Fearnley, Alie Benge, Airini Beautrais and Tracey Slaughter.

SUBMISSIONS CLOSE 31 JULY

OTAGO UNIVERSITY PRESS
Te Whare Tā o Te Wānanga o Ōtākou
oup.nz

For more information go to:
oup.nz/landfall-essay-comp

Dunedin's most loved independent book shop, full of beautiful books, elegant gifts, postal services and friendly booksellers.

378 Great King St
Dunedin North
03 477 6976
enquiries@unibooks.co.nz

Mon-Fri: 9am-5.30pm
Sat-Sun: 10am-4pm

www.unibooks.co.nz

LANDFALL
Young Writers' Essay Competition

Entries are now open for the 2024 **Landfall Young Writers' Essay**

The competition is open to anyone in Aotearoa aged 16–25 and will be judged by *Landfall* editor Lynley Edmeades.

The winner will receive $500 and a year's subscription to *Landfall*. They will also have their essay published in *Landfall 247*, coming out in May 2024.

ENTER NOW | Entries close 31 March 2024
Find out more at oup.nz/landfall-yw-essay-comp

CONTRIBUTORS

Pip Adam is the author of four novels: *Audition* (2023), *Nothing to See* (2020), *The New Animals* (2017) and *I'm Working on a Building* (2013); and the short story collection *Everything We Hoped For* (2010). She makes the *Better off Read* podcast.

Aimee-Jane Anderson-O'Connor is a writer living in Kirikiriroa. She is a keen zinester and collage maker and believes in the power of community and collaboration.

Jessica Arcus writes to give voice to the quiet and overlooked things and to draw out understanding from the inner thrashings. She has been published in the *Catalyst Literary Arts Journal* (2022), and the forthcoming *Aotearoa/NZ Performance Poetry Anthology* (Auckland University Press, 2023).

Rebecca Ball is a poetry and prose writer from Ōtautahi. She has had work published in journals and anthologies including *Landfall*, *London Grip*, *Turbine | Kapohau* and *Poetry Aotearoa Yearbook*.

Tony Beyer writes in Taranaki. His print titles include *Dream Boat: Selected poems* (HeadworX) and *Anchor Stone* (Cold Hub Press).

Victor Billot is a Dunedin writer. His poetry collection *The Sets* was published by Otago University Press in 2021. His poetry recently appeared in *A Kind of Shelter Whakaruru-taha: An anthology of new writing for a changed world* (Massey University Press, 2023).

Lucinda Birch is a writer and artist. She has had short stories published in *takahē*, *Jamm*, *Sport* and *Landfall*. In 2015 she won the Sunday Star Times Short Essay Competition. She lives in rural Wairarapa, a long way from the ocean.

Cindy Botha lives in Tauranga. Her poems have appeared in magazines and anthologies in the UK, Ireland, the USA, Australia and NZ.

Danny Bultitude is a Jewish Pākehā writer with his heart trapped in Porirua. His writing has appeared in *Ōrongohau | Best New Zealand Poems*, *Min-a-rets*, *The Spinoff* and many other publications.

Marisa Cappetta has published in journals and anthologies. *How to Tour the World on a Flying Fox* was published by Steele Roberts 2016. 'Tender Insurrections' is being published by Sudden Valley Press, November 2023.

Medb Charleton is originally from Ireland. Her poetry has been published previously in *Landfall* and *Sport*, among others. She is currently undertaking a PhD in English at the University of Waikato.

Janet Charman's *the pistils* (Otago University Press, 2022) was runner-up in the poetry category of the 2022 NZSA New Zealand Heritage Literary Awards and long-listed for the Ockham 2022 Best Book of NZ Poetry.

CONTRIBUTORS

Cadence Chung is a poet, student, composer and musician from Te-Whanganui-a-Tara, currently studying at the New Zealand School of Music. Her debut poetry book *anomalia* was published in April 2022 with Tender Press. She can be found weeping in antique stores.

Brett Cross lives in the Waikato where he runs two small publishing presses. He has previously published work in several journals, including *Cordite*, *Poetry NZ* and *Brief*.

Breton Dukes is the author of three collections of short stories. His last collection *What Sort of Man* came out during the 2020 Covid lockdown. He lives in Ōtepoti with his wife and three boys.

Mark Edgecombe lives in Tawa with Sarah and their children William, Elise and Bethany. Poems of his have appeared in *Landfall*, *takahē*, *Meniscus*, and *Quadrant*.

David Eggleton's *The Wilder Years: Selected Poems* was published by Otago University Press in 2021 and *Respirator: A Poet Laureate Collection 2019–2022* was published by Otago University Press in 2023.

Dr Rachel Faleatua has published on authenticity labour in *Continuum: Journal of Media & Cultural Studies* and has an upcoming book chapter on post vulnerability in *The Routledge Companion to Gender and Celebrity*.

Madeleine Fenn studied Classics at the University of Otago and is currently working towards an MA in Poetry at the Institute of Modern Letters. She is from Tairāwhiti.

Holly Fletcher is a dyslexic poet based in Ōtepoti. She studied at Goldsmiths University, London, where she gained a BA in Creative Writing. Her poetry has appeared in *Here Comes Everyone*, *Cherimus*, *Neo Gracie*, *The Spinoff*, *Otago Daily Times* and elsewhere.

Emma Gattey is a writer and critic from Ōtautahi. While working on a PhD in New Zealand History at the University of Cambridge, she is a Research Fellow for Te Takarangi at the University of Otago Faculty of Law and co-editor of The Pacific Circle.

John Geraets lives in Whangārei. His poetry collection *Everything's Something in Place* appeared from Titus Books in 2019. He curates the online journal *remake*.

Eliana Gray is a poet living in Ōtepoti. You can find their work in various places, both print and digital, such as *Landfall*, *Cordite*, *The Spinoff* and the *Poetry Aotearoa Yearbook*. Last week they swam with a stingray and loved it.

Jordan Hamel's debut poetry collection *Everyone is Everyone Except You*, published by Dead Bird Books in 2022, will be republished by Broken Sleep Books in the UK in 2024. He also co-edited *No Other Place to Stand*, an anthology of NZ climate change poetry (Auckland University Press, 2022). He is currently at the University of Michigan on a Fulbright Scholarship.

Siobhan Harvey is an estranged, emigre author of eight books, including *Ghosts* (2021) and Kathleen Grattan Award winner, *Cloudboy* (2014). Recently, her nonfiction essays have been published in *Fourth Genre* and *Griffith Review*.

Bronte Heron is a poet and educator born in Hāwera, currently based in New York City. They are an MFA candidate in the Creative Writing Program at the New School and an alum of the International Institute of Modern Letters. In 2022 they were a recipient of a General Graduate Award from Fulbright New Zealand.

Gail Ingram is an award-winning writer from Ōtautahi and author of *Some Bird* (Sudden Valley Press, 2023) and *Contents Under Pressure* (Pūkeko Publications, 2019). Her work has appeared widely here and overseas.

Lynn Jenner lives near Kerikeri. She has published three books: *Dear Sweet Harry* (Auckland University Press, 2010), *Lost and Gone Away* (Auckland University Press, 2015) and *Peat* (Otago University Press, 2019).

Erik Kennedy is the author of *Another Beautiful Day Indoors* (2022) and *There's No Place Like the Internet in Springtime* (2018), both with Te Herenga Waka University Press.

Megan Kitching lives in Ōtepoti. Her poetry has appeared in many publications including *Poetry New Zealand*, *takahē* and *Landfall*. Her debut collection is *At the Point of Seeing* (Otago University Press, 2023).

Jessica Le Bas has published two collections of poetry, *incognito* and *Walking to Africa* (Auckland University Press). In 2019 she won the Sarah Broom Poetry Prize, judged by Canadian poet, Anne Michaels. Her prescient children's novel *Locked Down* was re-released in 2021 by Penguin Random House. She now lives in Nelson, after some years in the Cook Islands.

Therese Lloyd lives in Wellington and grew up in Christchurch and Napier. She is the author of two collections of poetry, *Other Animals* (Victoria University Press, 2013) and *The Facts* (Victoria University Press, 2018) which was shortlisted for the Ockham Book Awards in 2019.

Mary Macpherson is a Wellington poet, photographer, photobook publisher and art writer. Her most recent poetry collection is *Social Media* (Cuba Press, 2019).

Carolyn McCurdie is a writer from Ōtepoti. Her first collection of poetry *Bones in the Octagon* was published by Mākaro Press in 2015.

Kirstie McKinnon lives, writes and surfs in East Coast Otago. She is inspired by conversation, nature and art. Her work has been published in *Otago Daily Times*, *takahē*, *Landfall*, *Corpus* and *Love in the Time of COVID*.

Frankie McMillan is an award-winning poet and short story writer. Her latest book, *The Wandering Nature of Us Girls*, was published by Canterbury University Press in 2022. Her work has been included in Best Microfiction and Best Small Fiction anthologies.

Zoë Meager's work has appeared in *Cheap Pop*, *Ellipsis Zine*, *Granta*, *Hue and Cry*, *Landfall*, *Lost Balloon*, *Mascara Literary Review*, *Mayhem*, *Meniscus*, *North & South*, *Overland*, *Splonk* and *Turbine | Kapohau*, among others.

Pam Morrison is a Dunedin-based writer of poetry and flash fiction. Her writing has been published in *Reflex* and *Bath Fiction* anthologies, *The New Zealand Listener*, *Meniscus* and *Flash Frontier*.

Petra Nyman is a Finnish-born writer who lives in Ōtautahi. She completed an MA in Creative Writing at the International Institute of Letters at Te Herenga Waka Victoria University of Wellington in 2020.

Jilly O'Brien is a psychologist from Ōtepoti. She has had poems published in *Landfall*, *Poetry New Zealand*, *Mayhem*, *takahē*, *Catalyst*, *The Spinoff*, *1964*, and overseas in *Cordite*, *Rabbit*, *Stand*, *The Blue Nib*, *Not Very Quiet*, as well as in a number of anthologies, on a bench and in Antarctica.

Vincent O'Sullivan writes across several genres. His most recent novella and short stories, *Mary's Boy, Jean-Jacques*, came out in 2022 (Te Herenga Waka University Press). Vincent lives in Dunedin.

Steven Junil Park is a multi-disciplinary artist based in Ōtautahi. He is known for his work under the name 6x4, where he produces one-off garments from second-hand materials.

Wendy Parkins is a writer based in Ōtepoti. Her memoir *Every Morning, So Far, I'm Alive* was published by Otago University Press in 2019. Her first novel, 'An Idle Woman', will be published by Legend Press in 2024.

Bronwyn Polaschek writes essays about things she's interested in. Most recently, she has published in *Headland* and was a writer for the Dirty Laundry show at Toi Pōneke. Bronwyn teaches at Onslow College.

Jenny Powell's most recent collection of poems is *Meeting Rita*, published in 2022 by Cold Hub Press. She is the Dunedin UNESCO City of Literature South D Poet Lorikeet, undertaking poetry projects in South Dunedin.

Rebecca Reader's work has been published in journals in New Zealand and overseas. Rebecca is a university writing consultant, a fiction reader for *takahē*, and a keen performer of Middle Eastern dance.

Pip Robertson has had stories published in journals and anthologies in Aotearoa and overseas. She lives in Wellington with her partner, daughter and dogs.

Reihana Robinson's published poetry volumes comprise *AUP New Poets 3* (Auckland University Press, 2008), *Auē Rona* (Steele Roberts, 2012), *Her Limitless Her* (Mākaro Press, 2018).

Tim Saunders was shortlisted for the 2021 Commonwealth Short Story Prize and is the author of two books: *This Farming Life* and *Under a Big Sky*.

Anna Scaife is a current MA student at the International Institute of Modern Letters at Te Herenga Waka Victoria University of Wellington. Anna's short fiction has appeared in *takahē* and the *Pure Slush 'Love' Anthology* (Bequem Publishing).

Iain Sharp is the author of five poetry books, *Real Gold: Treasures of the Auckland City Libraries* (Auckland University Press, 2007) and *Heaphy*, a biography of artist and explorer Charles Heaphy (Auckland University Press, 2008). In earlier times he edited the books pages for the *Sunday Star Times* and *Metro*. He now lives in Nelson.

Ann Shelton lives in Aotearoa New Zealand and exhibits internationally. Her most recent research engages with plants and plant narratives, in particular their intersection with human knowledge systems, feminisms and ecological politics. Her work is collected in public and private contexts throughout Aotearoa, Australia and North America.

Tessa Sinclair Scott gained her Creative Writing MA from the University of Sydney. In 2019 her poetry collection DREAM HOUSES was published by Kelsay Books in California. Tessa lives in Germany where she teaches and designs for culture and non-profits.

Mackenzie Smith is a writer living and working on unceded Gadigal Country. He grew up in Tāmaki Makaurau. His poetry has appeared in *Cordite*.

Elizabeth Smither's latest publication is *My American Chair* (Auckland University Press/MadHat USA, 2022). She is working on a collection of novellas.

Robert Sullivan (Ngāpuhi, Kāi Tahu, Irish) has won awards for his poetry, editing, and writing for children. His ninth collection of poetry, 'Hopurangi / Songcatcher' is forthcoming from Auckland University Press. Robert is an Associate Professor in Creative Writing at Massey University. He is a great fan of all kinds of decolonisation.

Catherine Trundle is a writer from Wellington, now living in Melbourne. Her poetry and flash fiction have appeared in a range of Australasian publications, including *Landfall*, *Not Very Quiet*, *Flash Frontier*, *takahē* and *Poetry Aotearoa Yearbook*.

Kathryn van Beek is the 2023 Burns Fellow and winner of the Mindfood Short Story Competition and the Headland Prize. Her work has appeared in *Overland*, *takahē*, *The Spinoff*, *Newsroom*, and in her short story collection, *Pet*.

Helen Watson White is a Dunedin writer with a background in university teaching, library work and editing. She has published a long list of reviews of theatre, books, music, art and opera, along with many articles, short stories, poems and photographs.

Sophia Wilson grew up in unceded Anaiwan country in Australia and now lives in rural Ōtepoti. Her first poetry collection *Sea Skins* was published by Flying Island Books/Cerberus Press in 2023.

Marjory Woodfield has had work published by the BBC, *Stuff*, and a range of literary journals and anthologies. She won the Robert Burns Poetry Competition in 2020. In 2022 she won the NZSA Heritage Poetry Award, was second in the Patricia Eschen Prize for Poetry, second in the NZFF Micro Flash Competition, highly commended in the Erbacce Prize for Poetry and shortlisted for the Cinnamon Literary Award.

Phoebe Wright is a writer of poetry and stories, currently living in Lyttleton and reading a lot of Denis Johnson.

Chris Yee works as an editor in Te Whanganui-a-Tara. His work has appeared in *Overcom* and *Headland*.

Wayne Youle (Ngāpuhi, Ngāti Whakaeke, Ngāti Pākehā) holds a Bachelor of Design from Wellington Polytechnic Design School and lives and works in Amberley, North Canterbury.

CONTRIBUTIONS

Landfall publishes original poems, essays, short stories, excerpts from works of fiction and non-fiction in progress, reviews, articles on the arts, and portfolios by artists. Submissions must be emailed to landfall@otago.ac.nz with 'Landfall submission' in the subject line.

For further information visit our website oup.nz/landfall

SUBSCRIPTIONS

Landfall is published in May and November. The subscription rates for 2024 (two issues) are: New Zealand $55 (including GST); Australia $NZ65; rest of the world $NZ70. Sustaining subscriptions help to support New Zealand's longest running journal of arts and letters, and the writers and artists it showcases. These are in two categories: Friend: between $NZ75 and $NZ125 per year. Patron: $NZ250 and above.

Send subscriptions to Otago University Press, PO Box 56, Dunedin, New Zealand. For enquiries, email landfall@otago.ac.nz or call 64 3 479 8807.

Print ISBN: 978-1-99-004864-7
ePDF ISBN: 978-1-99-004866-1
ISSN 00–23–7930

Copyright © Otago University Press 2023

Published by Otago University Press
533 Castle Street, Dunedin
New Zealand

Typeset by Otago University Press.
Printed in New Zealand by Caxton.

Steven Junil Park (6 x 4), *Untitled (Hanok)*, 2023.
Hand-carved limestone salvaged from the quake-demolished Christchurch basilica. Interior lined with 24K gold. Commissioned work by Objectspace for Octavia Cook's show: Cook & Company.